## SHAKESPEARE
### MADE IN CANADA

# The Tempest

## – WILLIAM SHAKESPEARE –

### GENERAL EDITOR: DANIEL FISCHLIN

OXFOR
UNIVERSITY PR

# OXFORD
### UNIVERSITY PRESS

Oxford University Press is a department of the University of Oxford.
It furthers the University's objective of excellence in research, scholarship,
and education by publishing worldwide. Oxford is a registered trade mark of
Oxford University Press in the UK and in certain other countries.

Published in Canada by
Oxford University Press
8 Sampson Mews, Suite 204,
Don Mills, Ontario M3C 0H5 Canada

www.oupcanada.com

**Library and Archives Canada Cataloguing in Publication**

Shakespeare, William, 1564–1616, author
The Tempest / William Shakespeare ; Daniel Fischlin,
general series editor.

(Shakespeare Made in Canada)
A play.
ISBN 978-0-19-900997-8 (pbk.)

I. Fischlin, Daniel, 1957–, editor of series II. Title.

PR2833.A2F58 2013      822.3'3      C2013-904342-X

Cover image: The Sanders Portrait of Shakespeare, 1603. By John Sanders. For more information
on what is now accepted as the only portrait of Shakespeare painted in his lifetime, see inside or
www.canadianshakespeares.ca.

Printed and bound in Canada.

1 2 3 4 — 16 15 14 13

MIX
Paper from
responsible sources
FSC® C004071

*In memory of Gerald J. Rubio*

*. . . of all sorts enchantingly beloved*
(*As You Like It* 1.1.139–40)

Christopher Plummer (Prospero), *The Tempest*, Stratford Festival, directed by Des McAnuff, 2010. Photograph: David Hou.

# Contents

# Ten Tips for Reading Shakespeare

1. **"Thou" vs. "You"**

   In the early modern period, "thou" was used when speaking to a social equal or a social inferior, whereas "you" was the more formal form of the second person pronoun. Think of it like "*tu*" and "*vous*" in French. For instance, in *Richard III*, when Richard is talking to Tyrell about the murder of the young princes, Richard—who is a king—uses "thou" and Tyrell—a commoner—uses "you."

2. **Original Pronunciation**

   The closest equivalent to early modern English pronunciation in contemporary Canada would be an outport Newfoundlander's accent. Vowels that we don't pronounce now were pronounced in early modern English, such that the suffix "-tion," for instance, was two syllables, not one. Many of Shakespeare's jokes and double entendres rely on the pronunciation he was familiar with— for instance, there is far more sexual connotation to the word "hour" when spoken in early modern English, where it was a homonym for "whore."

3. **Status**

   There was considerable social mobility in Shakespeare's day, meaning someone born poor could die rich and someone born rich could die poor. That social mobility caused anxiety for all, as the culture was ostensibly rigidly hierarchical. People began to insist upon "proper" etiquette. For example, in *Hamlet*, Osric the courtier repeatedly takes off his hat to Hamlet, indicating deference to him as his lord. Hamlet tells Osric to put his hat back on, leaving him to follow two different imperatives: the dictates of etiquette or Hamlet's own commands.

4. **Prosody . . .**

   . . . is the study of the metrical musical structures of language. Shakespeare generally wrote in "blank verse." "Blank verse" is simply unrhymed iambic pentameter poetry. An iamb is a unit of poetry where an unstressed syllable is followed by a stressed syllable. Pentameter means that there are five (penta) iambs per line (metre). Shakespeare used this as the baseline throughout his dramas, sometimes adding a syllable or breaking up the rhythm for effect. Beat out the lines with your fingers as you read and you will hear when Shakespeare is playing against/with the verse. Think of the play-text as a musical score with an intensely rich and rewarding set of possibilities for performance, depending on speech cadence, timbre, speed, emphasis, and other musical qualities that are key to the sonic effects Shakespeare scripted.

## 5.   Words, Words, Words

Recent computerized stylistic analysis has shown that Shakespeare actually created no more new words than any other playwright of his day.[1] It is just that his words caught on, while other playwrights' new words didn't. One of the ways in which Shakespeare "created" new words is through a device known as a "functional shift." These shifts occur when one kind of word (a noun, say) becomes another kind of word (a verb, for instance). An example from *Taming of the Shrew* is when Petruchio is described as being "Kated."

## 6.   Poetry vs. Prose

Sometimes characters speak in poetry, sometimes in prose. As a general rule, poetry indicates a kind of elevated speech, perhaps indicating the character is being polite, is of a high social status, or is engaging in witty repartee. Prose, on the other hand, tends to indicate characters of lower social status or "everyday" scenes. For example, in *Henry IV*, Prince Hal speaks in prose when he is with his lower-class friends, but in poetry when he is at the court.

## 7.   Vowels vs. Consonants

It is a good rule of thumb suggested by Patsy Rodenburg, head of voice at the Guildhall School of Music and Drama, that when you are reading aloud (and you should always read aloud), the consonants carry sense while the vowels carry emotion. Note when a certain vowel sound is held. For example, the sound of the words echoes the sense of them in *King Lear* when he says, "Howl! Howl! Howl! Howl! Howl!"

---

1   Hugh Craig, "Shakespeare's Vocabulary: Myth and Reality," *Shakespeare Quarterly* 62, no.1 (2011): 53–74.

## 8. Take Him Off the Pedestal

Stop thinking about Shakespeare as "the greatest writer of all time." Make up your own mind. If you don't like him, that's fine, but then you have to answer "why?" in a complex and thoughtful manner. Don't fall into the trap of thinking of Shakespeare as being very proper. Shakespeare wrote fart jokes and sex jokes, and he wrote about a good deal more of the human condition in sometimes earthy, sometimes elevated, ways. In some senses, Shakespeare's sense of humour was closer to the humour in *Family Guy* or *The Simpsons* than you might expect.

## 9. These Are Plays, Read Them as Plays

Plays have unique problems when you approach them as a text to-be-read rather than to-be-performed. For example, if someone does something significant in a novel, the author will usually spell it out in the narrative, but a playwright like Shakespeare doesn't need to waste the ink. Sometimes dialogue implies the actions of a scene in what are known as "internal stage directions." These editions have tried to point out some of the more obvious cases of internal stage direction but you should look for them everywhere.

## 10. Classical and Biblical References

Shakespeare came from a world steeped in the classics and the Bible. We do not. His audience would immediately have recognized references from classical learning and Biblical stories that we simply don't without help. Use the editorial notes to help you whenever you can. Always dig deeper if you have questions.

# A Dainty Dish before the King

## DANIEL DAVID MOSES

Was my first experience of *The Tempest* a fortunate one?

A summer theatre production, outdoors, with Haida-inspired design, despite the play's references to Milan, Algiers, and Roman myths, placed Prospero's island somehow off Canada's Pacific coast. A Cree actor played Caliban, a Kuna/Rappahannock actress the spirit Ariel. The play seemed then to be partly about Canada and colonialism, and with the creation story of the Haudenosaunee (Iroquois) already in my head—it tells that North America, Turtle Island, was created on a turtle's back by birds and animals eager to catch falling Sky Woman—the picture *The Tempest* proffered of a magus directing actions with the help of spirits on an island seemed familiar. It charmed me.

But now that I've read the play, I'm disappointed. It reads not like a masterwork but like a divertissement, short on story and characterization, though long on poetry, music, comedy, and spectacle. Prospero, the play's protagonist, I realize, being both a duke (though deposed) and magus enough to raise the storm that gives the play its title, is so powerful that the success of his plot to punish his usurpers, regain his dukedom, and set his daughter Miranda up in an honourable marriage is never in doubt. There's minimal suspense, the big conflicts are all past, and what passes for current ones are undeveloped (courtiers mutter about deposing the King of Naples but do nothing), or amount to little more than chiding (of his daughter Miranda or his favourite Ariel) or bullying (of his slave Caliban). The drama feels more abstract than active.

What's that about? Had the writer so famed for his plays and sonnets that he's now The Man, the genius of English literature, lost his edge or his ambition with this later play? Or was he having an off day?

That day would be more than four centuries back, close to the night *The Tempest* was first performed—on November 1, 1611, surviving records attest, in London for an audience centred on King James, who's best remembered for the publication that same year of the translation of the Bible that carries his name.

Was savvy Will Shakespeare writing for an audience of one who wouldn't appreciate even a fiction of treason? That Hallomas night, the magus with his book and staff on his lonely island must certainly have mirrored His Majesty's own royal isolation, wielding his Bible and rod over an ocean-bounded dominion. "Uneasy lies the head. . . ." Diverting the king with entertainment with a happy ending? Crafty strategy for keeping one's own head.

How much can we share in what held the king's attention when even his Bible is now out of fashion, congregations preferring scripture presented in lay language?

All but one of the play's characters are men, royalty, and their servants, slaves and spirits—and all of them, of course, including the spirit Ariel and even the virgin Miranda, were then played by men. The world the play originated in and represents as entertainment is one our democratic selves cannot approach without deliberation.

In our world—talk of a sea-change! (the word seems to have been coined in this play)—even a woman (Helen Mirren) has played the magus Prospera. And the voice of slave Caliban rings most clearly to my twenty-first century Iroquoian ears, singing drunkenly, hopefully, of freedom while Prospero yearns to go back to his dukedom. The duke isn't, after all, at home on the play's island or, perhaps, on this one.

Cast of *The Tempest*: *Forecast Disorder*, Gravy Bath Productions, directed by Madd Harold, 2001.

# "Where is Here?": Shakespeare, Canada, and The Tempest

## DANIEL FISCHLIN

### I

*The Tempest* famously opens with a "tempestuous noise of thunder and lightning" and a scene in which drowning at sea, the terror caused by inclement weather, and survival in a hostile environment set the stage for much of what is to follow. These images reflect on encounter and discovery narratives that were very much in the air when Shakespeare conceived, wrote, and staged the play in the early seventeenth century (circa 1610–12). On November 1, 1611, a performance was recorded at the Palace of Whitehall, the main residence of the English monarchs in London from 1530 until 1698. *The Tempest* was also part of the extended celebrations for the marriage of Elizabeth Stuart (also known as the Winter Queen), King James's third child and eldest daughter, to Frederick V, the Elector Palatine in 1612–13. Apart from *The Winter's Tale*, *The Tempest* is the only Shakespearean play to make weather a central, if not dominant, feature of its title; this in a host of plays where names—think Romeo, Juliet, Coriolanus, Titus Andronicus, and Hamlet—or pithy phrases—think *Much Ado About Nothing*, *A Comedy of Errors*, and *Measure for Measure*—dominate. Shakespeare's purported last play was also the first to appear in the 900-some page, 36-play, 1623 Folio edition edited by Henry Condell and John Heminges, both actors with Shakespeare in the King's Men, the theatre company that King James VI (later James I) had patronized in 1603 when he ascended the English throne on the death of Elizabeth I.

*The Tempest*, despite its designation as a romance that is light on plot and heavy on stagecraft, is perhaps Shakespeare's most emblematic play in matters related to both modernity and to the early modern period associated with Elizabethan and Jacobean cultures. Renaissance early modernity re-inscribed Classical sources in its literature and culture through learned citation and intertextual references in the movement known as Humanism. Yet *The Tempest* is decidedly modernist in its attention to encounter, exploration, and discovery narratives, largely derived from contemporary accounts of the same. Aside from envisaging a "brave new world" peopled by "many goodly creatures" in Miranda's famous phrase, *The Tempest* also depicted a threatening island world populated by a monstrous indigene (Caliban, the hybrid spawn of a witch and a demon); an ambiguously gendered and raced spirit creature (Ariel, an "airy spirit") along with multiple other spirits who populate the isle; a witch (Sycorax); and an inhospitable domain only made livable for the interlopers who come to the island by the intervention of Prospero's magical technologies, his book learning, and the supposed civilizing imperatives for which he stands. As a late play in Shakespeare's career, then, *The Tempest* straddles eras, emergent trends in colonial power relations, and knowledge systems in which technology and exploration were to play key roles.

Tropes of hostile environments and encounters with difference (that which we don't know or designate as other from what we know or find customary) are familiar to Canadians and form part of the stereotypical narratives associated with colonization of a vast, threatening land. Discovery narratives marked the "brave new world" as a menacing environment in which survival was, as renowned Canadian author Margaret Atwood notes in her seminal 1972 book *Survival*, a necessary aspect of settler reality. Atwood posits that the key question for Canadians is, "Where is here?"[1]—an unavoidable problem that arises when one finds oneself in "unknown territory,"[2] confronted with issues that pertain to survival: "Where is this place in relation to other places? How do I find my way around in it? . . . [is it] too hot, too cold, too wet or too dry . . . [are there] natives who are co-operative, indifferent or hostile[?]"[3] These questions, too, lie at the heart of what both Prospero, the usurped Duke of Milan, and Alonso, the King of Naples, must ask when they find themselves marooned on the enchanted, unnamed isle as a result of political subterfuge and magical incantation. The struggle to survive in a hostile environment governed by the elements, and the capacity of that environment to forge new forms of meaning, new forms of community, and new forms of power relations, makes *The Tempest* a particularly fascinating incubator of emergent encounter narratives—narratives that cannot be dissociated from Canada's own considerable colonial histories. Encounter narratives were a crucial aspect of how the discovery of the vastness and strangeness of the Americas precipitated literary responses that struggled to deal with the outlines of the new imaginary associated with unknown domains. New

---

1   Margaret Atwood, *Survival: A Thematic Guide to Canadian Literature* (Toronto: House of Anansi Press, 2013), 11.
2   Ibid.
3   Ibid.

geographies underlie new imaginative forms of addressing those geographies, something Shakespeare artfully demonstrates in *The Tempest*.

The encounter with difference, then, is at the core of what *The Tempest* explores in ways that complicate the stereotypical colonial narrative of settler superiority in the face of indigenous incompetence. If anything, *The Tempest* lays bare the manipulations of imperial power, emblematized in Prospero's subjugation of Ariel and Caliban—versions of unknowable forces and indigenous difference that were key constructs in discovery narratives of the time. At the same time, the play outlines an alternative vision of encounter based on the great French, early modern essayist Michel Eyquem de Montaigne's "Des cannibales" (Of the cannibals), published as chapter 30 in his first volume of *Les essais* (The essays), a major demonstration of Renaissance Humanist learning. The essay resulted from Montaigne's encounter with Brazilian Amerindians (supposed cannibals) who were visiting Rouen in 1563 at the invitation of King Charles IX.

Much has been made of Caliban as an anagram of "cannibal" and as a symbol of the dangerous unknowability of the indigenous other, whether cannibal or not. But it is worth emphasizing that Shakespeare's Caliban *never* engages in cannibalism, expressing instead a procreative imperative to people "this isle with Calibans" as justification for his attempted rape of Miranda. Caliban wishes to proliferate, not consume. By contrast, Prospero, in his enslavement of both Caliban and Ariel, cannibalizes their labours in order to reassert his political dominance. In both these examples, a key concept is hybridity: Caliban's desired miscegenation with Miranda hints at a future reality of crossbreeds, while Prospero's use of the labour of the island's indigenes suggests a codependent bond, one in which hybridized, exploitative relations determine the social and cultural realities of the island. The inevitability of hybridization that arises from discovery encounters, regardless of attempts to police intercultural exchanges so as to maintain the purity of either the settler or the indigene, is one of *The Tempest*'s uncanny insights into the drama of colonial encounter that was unfolding in the sixteenth and seventeenth centuries as a global phenomenon.

Inversion of expectation is typically Shakespearean, and asks that we not settle into easy stereotypes that are discordant with alternative, and often disruptive, realities—hence the Caliban or indigenous other who is *not* a cannibal; the supposedly civilized European patriarch who deploys his technologies of domination in exploitative ways that contradict notions of basic civility and egalitarian justice; and the encounter narrative that posits new social forms in the face of attempts to contain them. One of the great accomplishments of the play is to lay bare how European civil discourse masks brutal power struggles in which military force, Machiavellian political machinations, and technology determine who will be ascendant. Civil discourse in this context is predicated on who is most skilful at exercising power. This insight is one of the reasons why Caliban curses

Prospero, saying, "You taught me language; and my profit on't / Is, I know how to curse. The red plague rid you / For learning me your language!" The point here is that language, more specifically the language of Prospero, is a tool of oppression for Caliban: he is enslaved by its imperatives and by the wider cultural referents it evokes. Caliban has learned Prospero's language and is no slouch when it comes to using it to curse, even as Prospero does the same to him. Their language is the same yet different, inflected by their particular formations and world views, their particular relations to power, and the fact that both use it to gain "profit." The play, then, makes a point of showing the interconnected realities that emerge when the indigene learns the colonizer's discourse.

Prospero refers to Caliban as "slave," invokes his "vile race," and uses other forms of abusive language to denominate Caliban as an uncivilized other. And Caliban recognizes in Prospero's art "such power, / It would control my dam's god, Setebos, / And make a vassal of him." In such a context where slavery is clearly at issue, it is hardly a stretch to sympathize with Caliban while condemning Prospero's treatment of him. The unjust conditions of Caliban's enslavement are an invitation to question civil norms used to address cultural difference through fear, intimidation, and brute force. In the case of the sprite Ariel, it is the pregnant witch Sycorax who, abandoned on the island by sailors, imprisons Ariel in a tree "by help of her more potent ministers" before she dies. This occurs prior to Prospero's arrival on the island, when he frees but also re-enslaves Ariel by other means The island is thus a site where colonial gestures of enslavement recur, and where the use-value of its occupants is constantly being appropriated by settlers, whether by Sycorax (in the case of Ariel) or by Prospero (in the case of both Ariel and Caliban, and then later in the case of the survivors of the shipwreck).

The 1603 English translation of Montaigne's "Of Cannibals" by Shakespeare's contemporary John Florio (1553–1625) makes explicit a number of themes evident in *The Tempest*. The first is the power of what Montaigne calls "our great and puissant mother Nature."[4] Montaigne adds that we (meaning his European contemporaries) "have so much by our inventions surcharged the beauties and riches of her works, that we have altogether overchoaked her."[5] Earlier in the essay, Montaigne evokes the "corrupted taste" of Europeans, going so far as to talk of how European culture "bastard[izes]" the "naturall properties" of the new world. These paired motifs, of a powerful Mother Nature and of the ways in which so-called civil European culture debases her, are part of the emergent

---

4    Michel Eyquem de Montaigne, "Of the Caniballes," in *The Essays of Montaigne's Done into English by John Florio*, vol. 1 (London: David Nutt by the Strand, [1603] 1892), 221.

5    Ibid.

discourse of encounter in which *The Tempest* has played a prominent role. In *The Tempest*, nature is often a pejorative term referencing human nature, for instance, the "evil nature" of Prospero's "false brother" (1.2.192–96); Prospero's own distorted nature caused by his ill temper ("My father's of a better nature, sir, / Than he appears by speech" [1.2.495–96]); and Caliban's nature as a "devil, a born devil, on whose nature / Nurture can never stick" (4.1.188–89), emblematic of the stereotypical indigene who refuses to be "civilized." Nature, then, is not so much an external ecosystem as a referent for an internal landscape that is toxic, subject to human frailty.

By the end of the play, the word "nature" references a base state beyond which humanity ventures into unknowable terrain: "This is as strange a maze as e'er men trod / And there is in this business more than nature / Was ever conduct of. Some oracle / Must rectify our knowledge" (5.1.247–50). Here, the encounter between human invention and nature takes us into a realm that exceeds nature, requiring the special oracular, perhaps magical knowledge that Prospero (or the playwright Shakespeare) possesses in order to be understandable. The strange "maze" to which Alonso refers at the play's end exceeds nature and leads to "amazement"—quite literally (and etymologically) a state of being overwhelmed with "wonder"—a word that recurs three times at the end of *The Tempest*. Gonzalo declaims, in one instance, "All torment, trouble, wonder and amazement / Inhabits here. Some heavenly power guide us / Out of this fearful country!" (5.1.104–106. This is followed shortly thereafter by Miranda's exclamation, "O, wonder! / How many goodly creatures are there here? / How beauteous mankind is? O brave new world, / That has such people in't" (5.1.185–88). In both these cases "wonder" is associated with either "this fearful country" or the "brave new world," suggesting that the encounter of the human and the telluric (earthly) other is what precipitates new forms of knowledge. The collision of telluric, elemental forces and human invention that is also a form of intervention into the "natural" world, then, is a key aspect of the "new world" encounter narratives to which *The Tempest* belongs. It is within this frame that *The Tempest* lays out some of the key problems that originated in settler culture's encounter with indigenous peoples and environments it could not fully grasp.

Invention as intervention is very much in play in Montaigne's observation about "overchoak[ing]" nature with "inventions." The comment comes at the end of one of the most famous passages in the "Of Cannibals" essay where, rather than treating the "savage" cannibals as inferior to Europeans, Montaigne says,

> I finde (as farre as I have beene informed) there is nothing in that nation [of the cannibals], that is either barbarous or savage, unlesse men call that barbarism which is not common to them. As indeed, we have no other ayme of truth and reason, than the example and Idea of the opinions and customes of the country we live in. There is ever

perfect religion, perfect policie, perfect and compleat use of all things. They are even savage, as we call those fruits wilde, which nature of her selfe, and of her ordinarie progresse hath produced: whereas indeed, they are those which our selves have altered by our artificiall devices, and diverted from their common order, we should rather terme savage.[6]

The passage clearly identifies the dangers of self-centred ethnographies and of relative forms of knowledge derived using the norms of what "we" know as the basis for encountering difference. The rhetoric of this passage is rather extraordinary; the notion of the savage results from two sources: from the failure of so-called civil Europeans to grasp their own limited understanding of reality, and from the tyranny of the civil norms we know in perverting "truth and reason." Reversing the meaning of the savage, barbaric other from referencing the natural, unspoiled world to referencing the "artificiall devices" of European culture that alter and divert the common order is a key precept of Montaigne's prescient essay.

*The Tempest* sets up a confrontation between the "common order" of the isle and Prospero's artifices that change the nature of the isle's reality. With its references to a great fertile island, and its evocation of an idyllic commonwealth that Shakespeare famously uses as the source for Gonzalo's utopian reveries in *The Tempest*, Montaigne's essay creates a particularly critical tone for encounter narratives. Montaigne recognizes, if not idealizes, the notion of a pure otherness that is open to corruption via the artifice of European culture. Hence, the courtier's notions, much ridiculed in *The Tempest*, that if he were to settle the island and reign over it he would produce a commonwealth "by contraries" to those he already knows:

> I' th' commonwealth I would, by contraries,
> Execute all things, for no kind of traffic
> Would I admit; no name of magistrate;
> Letters should not be known; riches, poverty,
> And use of service, none; contract, succession,
> Bourn, bound of land, tilth, vineyard, none;
> No use of metal, corn, or wine, or oil;
> No occupation, all men idle, all,
> And women too, but innocent and pure;
> No sovereignty— . . .
> All things in common nature should produce
> Without sweat or endeavour. Treason, felony,

---

Ibid.

Sword, pike, knife, gun, or need of any engine
Would I not have, but nature should bring forth,
Of its own kind all foison, all abundance
To feed my innocent people.
. . .
I would with such perfection govern, sir,
T'excel the Golden Age. (2.1.133–53)

Gonzalo's anarchic world, in which "no sovereignty" prevails, does away with "tilth" and "bourn" (that is, with notions of cultivatable land divided by ownership boundaries), does away with technology, institutions, and even "letters," leaving innocence and purity to "bring forth" "all abundance" and "perfection." The image of the "Golden Age" with which Gonzalo ends is consistent with European notions of the Ages of Man and an *ur*-state of Arcadian, golden perfection when all beings were in harmonious relation with each other. But it also alludes to the Golden Age of discovery and exploration where the newly discovered territories of the Americas gave potential access to places where the Golden Age was still extant—a fount of potential that could give renewed life to stagnant, impoverished European states.

This kind of language was very much in the air in relation to the territories that would become Canada. Stephen Parmenius's 1582 Latin poem *De Navigatione* . . . (On navigation . . .), for example, exchanges the "barren body of Queen Elizabeth" with the "fruitful, (re)productive land of America . . . *De Navigatione*'s discussion of a contemporary Golden Age initiates a series of parallels in the poem that will ultimately link Queen Elizabeth with the abundant newfound land. By juxtaposing descriptions of Newfoundland and England, a structural characteristic of the poem, *De Navigatione* encourages the reader to substitute the New World for the Old."[7] *The Tempest*, too, asks that we compare old and new worlds, but very much from within the contexts of the new world itself. Moreover, in its elaboration of different ways of staging the encounter—whether by terror and force via the intervention of Prospero, or by wonder and appreciation via Miranda, or by resentment and resistance via Caliban, or comic mishap via Stephano and Trinculo, or utopic, idealistic ruminations via Gonzalo—*The Tempest* allows for, if not encourages, multiple interpretations of what it might mean to be placed in a situation of encounter. In the case of Parmenius, he was likely the first Hungarian to travel to North America, visiting the harbour of St. John's, Newfoundland, in 1583 aboard the English ship the *Swallow*, captained by Maurice Brown. Of the land around St. John's, Parmenius

---

7    Shannon Miller, *Invested With Meaning: The Raleigh Circle in the New World* (Philadelphia, PA: University of Pennsylvania Press, 1998), 106.

wrote on August 6, 1583, "What shall I say . . . when I see nothing but a very wildernesse?"[8] The Newfoundland wilderness, in other words, left Parmenius virtually speechless. Parmenius drowned later that month when the *Swallow* was shipwrecked in rough seas off the coast of either Sable Island or Cape Breton. The encounter in this prototypical story of a newcomer to Canadian shores evokes a sense of amazement and wordless wonder at the unknowable landscape. And Parmenius's story replays the basic plot elements of *The Tempest*, though with a tragic end, in terms of encounter with "nothing but a very wildernesse" upon an island in the process of settlement, and its uncanny prolepsis of the shipwreck that is so crucial to the plotline of *The Tempest*.

## II

*The Tempest*, then, cannot be separated from the encounter narratives that were rife in the early modern period—the context in which it was created. These narratives imagined new, unknown worlds and what it might mean to intervene in them. Nor are the territories of what would come to be known as Canada separable from the imaginative play of discovery narratives, literature, and theatrical spectacle. It is worth noting that Miranda's famous phrase, taken up by Aldous Huxley as the title of his dystopian novel *Brave New World* (first published in 1932), is actually referencing her discovery of people *like herself*, that is, of other Europeans, and is not referencing her sense of wonderment at the beings who already populate the island on which she has grown up. The "brave new world" is not so much the island itself as the island populated by the very culture that has spawned Miranda. Rather than demonizing the strange others from a world she has never known, she recognizes their "goodly," beautiful natures, an encounter response exactly at odds with how her father demonizes Caliban and subjugates both Caliban and Ariel using the threat of ongoing torture or incarceration. This edition maintains the First Folio's use of a question mark after Miranda's line "How beauteous mankind is?" as an apt reflection of the ambiguities the play puts into question about the ethics of encounter narratives where human morality is tested.

Subtly, then, Shakespeare manages to link the more traditional form of colonial encounter (where all-knowing, superior beings encounter ignorant savages) with the Montaignean version in which encounter becomes a chance to recognize settler culture's limitations and biases when faced with forms of difference never seen before. In reading the play as an allegory of encounter it is important to note that geographically it is set in the Mediterranean, "an island somewhere

8   *Dictionary of Canadian Biography Online*, s.v. "Parmenius, Stephanus," by David B. Quinn, accessed April 12, 2013, http://www.biographi.ca/EN/009004-119.01-e.php?id_nbr=503.

between Tunis and Naples," as the great Canadian critic Northrop Frye points out.[9] Yet the play repeatedly evokes other forms of encounter narratives associated with cross-Atlantic discovery narratives. Frye himself evinced puzzlement at "why New World imagery should be so prominent in *The Tempest*, which really has nothing to do with the New World, beyond Ariel's reference to the 'still-vex'd Bermoothes' (1.2.230) and a general, if vague, resemblance between the relation of Caliban to the other characters and that of the American Indians to the colonizers and drunken sailors who came to exterminate or enslave them."[10] Nonetheless, Frye too recognizes how "the historical future in *The Tempest* is not obvious; but every editor of the play is compelled to deal . . . with the pamphlets and other documents that Shakespeare used about voyages across the Atlantic and to the New World, in spite of the fact that the play itself never goes outside the Mediterranean Sea."[11]

Even in Montaigne's essay there was considerable geographical confusion and speculation about an island that "should be the new world we have lately discovered; for, it well-nigh touched Spaine, and it were an incredible effect of inundation, to have removed the same more than twelve hundred leagues . . . Besides, our modern Navigations have now almost discovered, that it is not an Iland, bur rather firme land, and a continent, with the East Indies on one side, and the countries lying under the two Poles on the other."[12] The merging topographies associated with early modern exploration were, to say the least, muddled—and Shakespeare's *The Tempest* reflects hybridized imaginings about what these topographies might have looked like. During the very period in which *The Tempest* was written, the English explorer Henry Hudson was in a futile search for a passage to Asia through the waterways that eventually led him to "discover" and explore Hudson's Bay (circa 1610–11). Further, even as *The Tempest* tells, at least in part, the story of encounter between settler and indigene, the primary source material on which it was based is an English expedition shipwrecked on an island without people. Shakespeare's great insight was to imagine the shipwreck as generative of encounter with difference. The island is a metaphor or allegory for a world elsewhere, an undefined space in which the dynamics of encounter could be brought to life in ways that were true to both European and emergent new world realities, whatever the actual source of the idea was.

9   Northrop Frye, "Introduction to Shakespeare's *Tempest*," in *Northrop Frye's Writings on Shakespeare and the Renaissance*, ed. Troni Y. Grande and Garry Sherbert, vol. 28 of *The Collected Works of Northrop Frye* (Toronto: University of Toronto Press, [1959] 2010), 50.

10  Ibid., 51.

11  Northrop Frye, *The Myth of Deliverance: Reflections on Shakespeare's Problem Comedies* (Toronto: University of Toronto Press, 1983), 58.

12  Montaigne, "Of the Caniballes," 219.

Frye keenly observes in his 1959 introduction to the Penguin edition of *The Tempest* that the opening storm scene signals "a dissolving society" because the storm has no heed for the fact that is it is "afflicting a king"[13] and his royal retinue. Nature is the great leveller, a threat to order and stability. But in Shakespeare's subtle telling, it is especially nature manipulated by "man" that has the potential to undo kings and the power they exercise. Even as the royal society of Naples dissolves, then, Prospero's governance of the isle and all those who populate it consolidates itself, if only temporarily, using force, intimidation, technology (his magic), and artful stratagems based on surveillance and the manipulation of the island's indigenous inhabitants.

Frye's infamous notion of the "garrison mentality" is useful here as it so neatly describes early Canadian settler contexts in ways that adapt easily to the situation of *The Tempest*. In "characterizing the way in which the Canadian imagination was developed in its literature," Frye imagines "small and isolated communities surrounded with a physical or psychological 'frontier,' separated from one another and from their American and British cultural sources."[14] Frye sees the garrison as "a closely knit and beleaguered society, and its moral and social values are unquestionable. In a perilous enterprise one does not discuss cause or motives: one is either a fighter or a deserter."[15] Further, Frye argues that the garrison mentality, as it shifts "from the fortress to the metropolis," inevitably produces a literature that "tends to be rhetorical, an illustration or allegory of certain social attitudes."[16]

These ideas map onto *The Tempest* in uncanny ways. The isolation of the island separates Miranda from her own cultural sources. Her "home and native land" is, so to speak, a place she has no real knowledge of, leading to the un-naturally dependent, cloistered relation to her father and his machinations to restore himself to power. At the core of *The Tempest* are questions about how to define human community and about the ethics and moral purpose of the different groups on the island. Moreover, the play asks that we reconsider facile notions of identity linked to place: Miranda both *is* and is not of the isle; both *is* and is not of Milan. It is her very in-between-ness and her alienation that make her so troubling of simplistic notions of stable identity. The play very much puts into question Atwood's notion that "the collective hero can be an expression of a closed and ingrown garrison mentality or of a living community; collective

13   Frye, "Introduction," 44.
14   Northrop Frye, "Conclusion to the First Edition of *Literary History of Canada*," in *Northrop Frye on Canada*, ed. Jean O'Grady and David Staines, vol. 12 of *The Collected Works of Northrop Frye* (Toronto: University of Toronto Press, [1965] 2003), 350–51.
15   Ibid., 351.
16   Ibid., 355.

action [in Canada] has been necessary for survival but it may also stifle individual growth."[17] Prospero, as symbolic of the collective hero cast into the wilderness
of the island, is at once beleaguered but made stronger in his intent by that sense
of disempowerment. By holding true to the new terms of cultural and political
bonds the island affords him, he sets the stage for his return to power. But in so
doing Prospero also reproduces the colonial logic of subjugation and false unity
that is a key element in the play—and a key element in the stifling of Miranda's
broader knowledge of the world around her.

The play's allegory of isolation and encounter, of beleaguered paranoia and
codependency, of the hybridized, collided realities of the island and its strange
mirroring of mainland society, all tell us that Shakespeare is at work with a
deeply allegorical literary structure with multiple levels of interpretation that address the social attitudes towards otherness, difference, alienation, power, and
reconciliation. Fantasy, mystery, illusion, faulty perception, and unknowing are
all key imaginative devices in the play. The early-twentieth-century Canadian
critic Orlando John Stevenson, head of the English Department at the Ontario
Agricultural College from 1919 to 1939 (now integrated into the University of
Guelph)—who between 1915 and 1943 edited the *Canadian School Shakespeare
Series*, which went on to sell over a million copies through its publisher Copp
Clark, one of Canada's oldest publishing companies—notes how closely tied are
the mystery and the unknown in the play. Stevenson argues, "in *The Tempest*
the audience can never escape from this mystery. Behind the magic of Prospero
there lies the great unexplored realm of spiritual influences and spiritual presences which holds us under its spell."[18] However true this is, the play also makes
explicit the underlying dangers of abusive interventions into this mysterious
space via vain sorcery, cheap wizard's tricks. Prospero tells Ariel in 4.1 to "Go,
bring the rabble— / O'er whom I give thee power—here to this place. / Incite
them to quick motion, for I must / Bestow upon the eyes of this young couple /
Some vanity of mine art." The lines are telling. The hierarchy of power is explicit
with Prospero giving Ariel the capacity to assemble what he calls the "rabble," the
lesser spirits of the isle. Prospero's first gift to the lovers is "Some vanity of mine
art," as if to suggest that he has little respect for the "rabble" (the disorderly mob)
who are to help him create his conjurations, and as if to suggest that the lovers
merit little more than an artful vanity.

The strategic displays of power mask attitudes that do not bode well for
the reconciliatory gestures towards which the play moves. The play's epilogue,

---

17   Atwood, *Survival*, 193.
18   Orlando John Stevenson, *Shakespeare's The Tempest. With Annotations by O. J. Stevenson*
     (Toronto: Copp Clark, 1927), xiv.

spoken by Prospero, underlines that "Now I want / Spirits to enforce, art to enchant, / And my ending is despair." These lines suggest that power is very much constructed out of art, enchantment, and dependent relations without which Prospero cannot come to a happy end. Moreover, Prospero's last appeal is to "be relieved by prayer." But this prayer, as Canadian critic Mark Fortier cannily observes, is "represented as a violence, a piercing and an assault"[19]: "And my ending is despair, / Unless I be relieved by prayer, / Which pierces so that it assaults / Mercy itself and frees all faults" (Epilogue 15–18). Allegorically laying bare the artifices of power and how it creates itself through spectacular devices and stagecraft, hidden dependencies that allow it to be enforceable, and violent strategies of repression, is very much at the core of how *The Tempest* makes its allegorical meanings about encounter relevant.

Regardless of the marriage, then, with the union of Ferdinand and Miranda as a supposed happy dénouement to the play that supposedly reconciles the warring brothers and frees Ariel and Caliban from their enslavement, the problem *The Tempest* leaves hanging is very much linked to how "unnatural" (5.1) unity in a family or community can sustain itself. As Frye put it in his canny read of Canada as a colonial entity, "Assimilating identity to unity produces the empty gestures of cultural nationalism."[20] That is, forced notions of alliance to a common identity, as with what happens to Ariel and Caliban or with Prospero and his brother in *The Tempest*, ultimately produce unstable, empty gestures of solidarity—even if forgiveness and reconciliation appear to occur. Encounter leads to questions about adaptation to new circumstances, but also to how these new circumstances affect our relations with the precedent histories to which we are unavoidably tied. Frye sagely observes that "every responsible citizen . . . must be concerned with finding means of adaptation to change, and therefore . . . must also be concerned with finding the pattern of continuity at the centre of change."[21]

But what are the prospects of a culture that finds reconciliation through intimidation, subjugation, and encounters based on differential powers and technologies? *The Tempest* asks us to consider these questions as part of its overall context within larger discourses of colonial encounter and discovery in which

19   Mark Fortier, "'In No Recognizable Way' *The Tempest*," in *Negation, Critical Theory, and Postmodern Textuality*, ed. Daniel Fischlin (Dordrecht: Kluwer, 1994), 76.

20   Northrop Frye, "Preface to *The Bush Garden*," in *Northrop Frye on Canada*, ed. Jean O'Grady and David Staines, vol. 12 of *The Collected Works of Northrop Frye* (Toronto: University of Toronto Press, [1971] 2003), 414.

21   Northrop Frye, "Foreword to *The Prospect of Change*," in *Northrop Frye on Canada*, ed. Jean O'Grady and David Staines, vol. 12 of *The Collected Works of Northrop Frye* (Toronto: University of Toronto Press, [1965] 2003), 373.

similar realities ineluctably led to the tensions that underlie much of the relations evident in the play. Fortier identifies violence "facilitated by magic" as a key feature of *The Tempest*. The technologies of violence that Prospero deploys are also tied by Fortier to "a growing body of criticism of the play concerned with the way the island stands in for the New World, and with the play's relation to the history and ideology of colonialism."[22] And Canadian critic Susan Bennett has underlined how "no Western text has played a more visible role in the representation and reconstruction of the colonial body than Shakespeare's *The Tempest*,"[23] suggesting that Prospero and Caliban are even "tired" tropes of settler and indigene. However tired the tropes are, they are nonetheless part of a long history of such imaginings that have helped shape encounter narratives.

Even the early Scottish-Canadian critic Sir Daniel Wilson (1816–92), first president of the federated University of Toronto (1890–92) and author of *Caliban, the Missing Link* (1873), felt compelled to explore the figure of Caliban as Shakespeare's anticipation of "Darwin's theory of evolution by nearly 300 years. For Wilson, Shakespeare's creation of the misshapen Caliban offered clear evidence of the Bard's intuitive grasp of evolutionary theory; Caliban was surely the 'missing link.'"[24] Wilson went so far as to argue that Caliban, "so far from being either superficial or repulsive . . . is a character which admits of the minutest study, and is wrought to the perfection of a consistent ideal not less harmoniously, and even beautifully, than Ariel himself. Both are supernatural beings, called into existence by the creative fancy of the poet; but the grosser nature is the more original of the two."[25] It is worth remembering that these interpretations of Caliban's "grosser nature" connect to brutal material realities that were being lived in the territories that were to become known as Canada in virtually the same moment as *The Tempest* came into existence. To cite but one example, in the case of the Aboriginal indigenes of Newfoundland, the Beothuk, their 1613 response to a gunfire attack on them—which resulted in the deaths of thirty-seven French fishermen—led to an alliance between the French and the Mi'kmaq, traditional enemies of the Beothuk. The Beothuk were then almost completely wiped out in the events that ensued shortly thereafter, an early instance of the genocide of indigenes associated with colonization. In this context, Shakespeare's only use in his entire body of work of the phrase "dead Indian," spoken by Trinculo in 2.2,

22  Fortier, "'In No Recognizable Way,'" 64–65.
23  Susan Bennett, "The Post-colonial Body? Thinking through *The Tempest*," in *Performing Nostalgia: Shifting Shakespeare and the Contemporary Past* (London: Routledge, 1996), 119.
24  Irena R. Makaryk, "'Wider Still and Wider': Societies and Universities," in "Shakespeare in Canada: 'A World Elsewhere'?" *The Internet Shakespeare*, accessed April 12, 2013, http://internetshakespeare.uvic.ca/Library/Criticism/shakespearein/canada4.html.
25  Sir Daniel Wilson, *Caliban: The Missing Link* (London: Macmillan and Co., 1873), 64.

has uncanny and poignant resonances within the emerging material realities of colonial encounter.

Specific sources of the encounter narratives at the core of the play include a number of early modern accounts of exploration of the Americas, in which English seafaring and the drive to find new economic opportunities linked to England's imperial imperatives were paramount. In 1610, Shakespeare may well have had access to, among others: William Strachey's *A true reportory of the wracke, and redemption of SIR THOMAS GATES knight*, published in 1625 by Samuel Purchas but in private circulation well before then as a letter written on July 15, 1610, to an anonymous "Excellent Lady" (the letter was suppressed by the Virginia Company because it was so critical of how the Jamestown colony was being administered); *Jourdain's Discovery* (whose full title was *A Discovery of the Barmudas, otherwise called the Ile of Divels: By Sir Thomas Gates, Sir George Sommers, and Captayne Newport, with diuers others. Set forth for the loue of my Country, and also for the good of the Plantation of Virginia*); the anonymous pamphlet *A True Declaration of the Estate of the Colonie in Virginia, With a Confutation of such scandalous Reports as have tended to the disgrace of so worthy an enterprise*; and the ballad *Riches Newes from Virginia* (full title, *Newes from Virginia, The Lost Flocke triumphant, with the happy Arriual of that famous and worthy knight, [Sir] Thomas Gates, and the well reputed and valiant Captaine Mr. Christopher Newporte, and others, into England, With the manner of their distresse in the Hand of Deuils (otherwise called Bermoothawes* [Bermudas]), *where they remayned 42 weekes and builded two Pynaces* [pinnace or small boat] *in which they returned into Virginia*.

These elaborate titles tell a fascinating story about the 1609 colonial expedition led by Sir George Somers, who set sail from England with nine ships and over 500 settlers bound for the "new world" of Virginia. With their evocation of an island of devils (the "Ile of Divels"), of unabashed patriotism ("loue of my Country"), of scandalous reports, of disgrace, of shipwreck and "redemption," and ultimately of English resourcefulness in the face of adversity, the titles outline narrative elements that Shakespeare uses throughout his play. One of the boats, the *Sea Venture* or *Sea Adventure*, with both Somers and Sir Thomas Gates on board, was wrecked off the Bermuda islands, with some 142 survivors making their way to safety on one of the islands. Then, after ten months of survival on the island, they built two cedar boats to continue their journey, eventually reaching Jamestown, Virginia. The adventure caught the imagination of the Jacobean public, especially when some of the survivors returned to England in 1610. Gates was the governor of Jamestown, named after King James VI/I, and is perhaps most famous for his involvement in the saga of Pocahontas, the Indian "princess" kidnapped in 1613 and converted to Christianity. Sir George Somers was the admiral of the Virginia Company, which included two joint stock companies (the London and Plymouth Companies) that King James had chartered in 1606 with the purpose of settling the east coast of North America. In roughly the same period, other equally impressive ventures associated with exploration and colonization were taking place further north in the vast new world territories that would eventually become Canada. In these contexts, *The Tempest* can be understood as part of a narrative continuum imagining the perils of exploration, the challenges of settlement, and the underlying profit-seeking (the "prosperity" perhaps figured in Prospero's name) associated with colonization and the corporations involved therein.

## III

*The Tempest* has been played and replayed in Canada in multiple ways that reflect on the colonial encounter and discovery narratives discussed in this essay. It is important to underline that whether in productions or in adaptations, Canada has a history of playing and adapting *The Tempest* in ways that figure distinctly Canadian realities, but that this connection is not always present or even necessary—and that other thematic concerns of the play also get addressed as a result of different interpretative frames. These production practices are too diverse to be comprehensively addressed here. Nonetheless a few thought-provoking examples are worth considering.

Canadian director Lewis Baumander's 1989 production in Earl Bales Park, Toronto, staged by Skylight Theatre, was

> set on the Queen Charlotte Islands, off the British Columbian coast, at the time of their colonization. Without altering the text, Baumander presents a New World interpretation of the conflict that results when a harmonious indigenous culture is forced to accommodate an encroaching alien presence. Designer William Chesney took his inspiration from the visually rich culture of the west coast Haida Indians and created a set to blend with the natural beauty of Earl Bales Park. Cree Choreographer Rene Highway's movement is a combination of modern and Native dance styles. Baumander and Skylight Theatre seek to explore the issues surrounding native peoples everywhere, and more specifically to celebrate Canada's heritage via the cultures of its indigenous peoples.[26]

The Baumander production produced conflicted responses, not the least because Cree actor Billy Merasty, a nephew of well-known Cree playwright Tomson

---

26  Lewis Baumander, cited in Daniel Fischlin, "The Tempest," *Canadian Adaptations of Shakespeare Project*, accessed April 14, 2013, http://www.canadianshakespeares.ca/Production_Shakespeare/SearchPublicShowPlay.cfm?PlayID=651.

Highway (and later a member of the 2012 all-Aboriginal cast of *King Lear* staged at Canada's National Arts Centre in Ottawa), played Caliban as a stereotypical drunken buffoon. Merasty's depiction of Caliban via Baumander's direction did not, as Helen Peters opined, "appear to challenge the authority of the imperial power [Prospero] . . . or to threaten its overthrow."[27] Where Merasty played to stereotypes, Monique Mojica, of Kuna and Rappahannock ancestry, played a "trickster-inspired" Ariel who, in Bennett's read, "laid bare in Prospero his otherwise uncontested assumptions of symbolic legitimacy and intelligibility."[28]

Further, critic Paul Leonard notes how the attempt to "make Shakespeare relevant to Canadians in the 1980s presupposes that there is (at least) a kernel of meaning in the works that applies to Canada . . . Unfortunately, much as we may enjoy celebrating Shakespeare as a Canadian, that is to say 'universal' playwright, we cannot make him one of us. Instead, we must make ourselves into him."[29] In this context, Baumander's production becomes for Leonard a "denial of difference in favour of an expression of commonality" that is severely at odds with the "ideology of the original play . . . specific to a culture—Jacobean England—which was embarking on the program of colonization that would lead to the British Empire."[30] Understood in this light, Baumander's reading, in spite of its apparent solidarity with the Haida culture it is representing, in fact "appropriates the culture and struggle of native people to propagate an imperialistic vision."[31] The very Canadianization of the play's contexts, then, stages some of the tensions that arise in colonial culture, where iconic symbols of colonial influence and imperial power like Shakespeare are in troubled relation to the legacy of oppression they are supposedly addressing.

In 2011, some twenty-two years later, the Québécois director and dramaturge Robert Lepage and his production company Ex Machina staged a collaborative version of Shakespeare's *The Tempest* (*La Tempête*, in a translation by multi-talented Québécois author and performer Michel Garneau), in the intercultural setting of the First Nations (Huron-Wendat) village of Wendake. Ex Machina's press release about the production was explicit, with the play described as "a true meeting place . . . A cultural encounter between Natives and non-Natives" that brought "together different generations and forms of expression."[32] The allegory of colonial first contact plays out in Lepage's version of the play in startling new

---

27  Cited in Bennett, "The Post-colonial Body," 140.
28  Ibid.
29  Paul Leonard, "*The Tempest* x 2 in Toronto," *Canadian Theatre Review* 54, no. 4 (1988): 11.
30  Ibid.
31  Ibid., 12.
32  "*La Tempête*, Directed by Robert Lepage in July 2011," Ex Machina press release, 2011.

ways that depend on the actual First Nations setting in which the play was staged. Lepage deployed Huron-Wendat actors dressed in traditional garb and speaking their language in the production. Steeve Wadohandik Gros-Louis played King Alonso of Naples, as an instance of this multicultural mix-up, and Gros-Louis's well-known dance troupe, Sandokwa (meaning "eagle"), played a key role in the production, an intervention remarkable for how it made evident the cultural spaces the production was intermixing. Of note in both these productions is the staging in outdoor spaces, a distinctive feature of Canadian Shakespeare productions, and Canadians' putative "preference for Shakespeare paired with a beautiful landscape. Since the 1980s, boisterous summer Shakespeare is found not only *a mari usque ad mare* (Wolfville, Halifax, St. John's, Montreal, Toronto, Saskatoon, Victoria, Vancouver, and, briefly, Ottawa), but also by the sea, in a park, or on a golf course."[33]

Lepage's production was, in part, "inspired by a Joseph Légaré painting (c. 1826), 'Edmund Kean Reciting Before the Hurons,' that depicts Edmund Kean (1787–1833), the famous English actor, performing Shakespeare in Wendake in the 1800s. Légaré (1795–1855) was a prominent artist, seigneur, and politician in Lower Canada known for his depictions of First Nations peoples and their customs and Kean was much admired by the Hurons who made him an honorary chief and gave him the name 'Alanienouidet,' meaning 'strong wind in drifting snow.'"[34] The through-line from Kean and his connection to English productions of Shakespeare, to Légaré's visual depiction of Kean in a multicultural (French Canadian and First Nations) Canadian context, through to Lepage's contemporary restaging in light of all these antecedent cultural collisions via various media tells a remarkable story about how the narratives of encounter that are so crucial to *The Tempest*'s story have travelled in distinctly Canadian contexts. That *The Tempest* also dates to the approximate founding of Lepage's hometown, Quebec City, in 1608 by Samuel de Champlain, further demonstrates how theatrical representations from within a specific national site can heighten and amplify historical relations. Not only is Quebec one of the oldest cities in the Americas but its name derives from *kepék*, an Algonquin word for "[it] narrows" (also "strait"), a reference to how the St. Lawrence River narrows where the city of Quebec was founded—facts that further deepen the play of historical context in Lepage's 2011 production.

---

33 Irena R. Makaryk, "Canada," in *The Oxford Companion to Shakespeare*, ed. Michael Dobson and Stanley Wells (Oxford: Oxford University Press, 2001), 64.

34 Marie White Windspeaker, "Huron-Wendat Village of Wendake Stage *The Tempest*," *AMMSA* 29, no. 6 (2011), accessed May 30, 2013, http://www.ammsa.com/publications/windspeaker/huron-wendat-village-wendake-stages-tempest.

Lepage has been involved in multiple productions and adaptations of *The Tempest*, including a 2012 production of British composer Thomas Adès's operatic adaptation. Lepage's concept for the production entailed Prospero as a tattooed eighteenth-century opera impresario whose manipulations of the people on the isle paralleled that of an opera director manipulating his or her cast. The conceit is familiar: the play is the text on which the director overlays a concept that makes it even more realized, even more of an invention. Often such inventions have a great deal to do with the cultural formations and conditions in which one lives. Hence, in yet another *Tempest*-related staging involving Lepage, Canadian critic Paul Yachnin has shown how in the "1993 production of [*The Tempest*] at the Festival de Théâtre des Amériques in Montreal, Caliban was [portrayed as] a punk rocker whose colloquial 'joual' French, set off against Prospero's formal diction, captured the persistence of class differences in modern Quebec."[35]

Yachnin further reminds us that not all productions necessarily reflect on the politics of the play: "In the Canadian Stratford Festival production of 2010, starring Christopher Plummer, the figure of Caliban was an empty vestige of the previous century's engagement with the political meanings of the servant monster. The focus shifted to the girlish, blue Ariel, a witty and tender figure that held Prospero's heart just as she held his."[36] Yachnin further notes how "the Stratford *Tempest* . . . suggests something about the fate of art in modernity. As a commercial artwork such as *The Tempest* becomes more visible, more available to a mass market, and more able to move from one media form to another, it becomes correspondingly less capable of speaking creatively about matters of shared concern and less able to foster public debate, judgment, or action."[37] These are but a few examples from many such Canadian re-envisionings, adaptations, and devisings in which Shakespeare is implicated. The key is to understand Shakespeare's brand recognition as a focus, for better or worse, of refashionings that arise from the specific national contexts in which debates like these are played out in theatrical spectacle.

The visual imagination that is so crucial to Lepage's theatrical mash-ups is also part of how notions of adaptation travel culturally. In the case of visual representations created in Canada that link *The Tempest* to First Nations realities, Western Canadian Metis artist David Garneau's 2003 painting *Riel/Caliban*, from his series *Cowboys and Indians (and Métis?)*, is, as he puts it in his artist's notes to the image,

---

35   Paul Yachnin, "*The Tempest*: Critical Introduction," *The Internet Shakespeare*, accessed April 12, 2013, http://internetshakespeare.uvic.ca/Annex/Texts/Tmp/intro/GenIntro/default/.

36   Ibid.

37   Ibid.

a familiar portrait of Louis Riel with the addition of a cartoon "thought balloon" leading off the canvas. The idea is that a viewer is looking at Riel and thinking "Caliban." . . . I imagine someone relating to Riel as Prospero related to Caliban . . . like Caliban, Riel's romantic interest in a white woman was rejected by her father. Like Caliban, Riel was "country born" but raised within the (French Catholic) dominant culture ideology, educational and religious system . . . The Metis, like Caliban, "show'd thee all the qualities o' the [prairies], The fresh springs, brine-pits, barren place and fertile . . ." In my fantasy, Prospero and Sycorax are Caliban's parents, making him Metis! There is a familiar inter-racial anxiety in the play. Prospero worries about a connection between Caliban and Miranda . . . In this sense, the Metis might be seen as "Calibans" . . .[38]

Louis Riel (1844–85) was the executed Metis leader who founded modern-day Manitoba and headed the resistance movement against Prime Minister John A. MacDonald's colonial policies in the Canadian West. MacDonald was behind the notorious 1879 *Davin Report*, which instituted a racist, assimilationist federal policy and set the stage for creation of the notorious residential schools system in Canada that has played such a destructive role in the history of its First Nations peoples. In such a context, Garneau's association of Riel and Caliban reinvigorates the symbolic resonance of what Shakespeare signifies and how those significations continue to produce new, provocative meaning in Canada.

Many other adaptations and productions of *The Tempest* occur in specific Canadian contexts. Distinguished Canadian author Robertson Davies's 1951 first novel *Tempest-Tost*, also the first book in his *Salterton Trilogy*, famously relies on Davies's own experience with Canadian community theatre. Written just four years after Canada's Canadian Citizenship Act came into effect—an act that made Canadian citizenship independent from British nationality—the novel tells of an amateur production of *The Tempest*, albeit with some very specific lines that address what it might mean to be Canadian:

> "I wanted to get away," said she; "everybody wants to plague and worry me about nothing. They'll be all right tomorrow. What's worrying them?"
>
> "They are sacrificing to our Canadian God," said Solly. "We all believe that if we fret and abuse ourselves sufficiently, Providence will take pity and smile upon anything we attempt. A light heart, or

---

38   David Garneau, cited in Daniel Fischlin, "David Garneau," *Canadian Adaptations of Shakespeare Project*, accessed April 14, 2013, http://www.canadianshakespeares.ca/multimedia/imagegallery/m_i_2.cfm.

a consciousness of desert, attracts ill luck. You have been away from your native land too long. You have forgotten our folkways. Listen to that gang over there; they are scanning the heavens and hoping aloud that it won't rain tomorrow. That is to placate the Mean Old Man in the Sky, and persuade him to be kind to us. We are devil-worshippers, we Canadians, half in love with easeful Death. We flog ourselves endlessly, as a kind of spiritual purification."[39]

Davies's caricature of dour Canadians trapped by providential thinking hints at the uses of Shakespeare to define a national imaginary. Indeed, the novel has been read as "a Canadian parody of *The Tempest*, which explores the anxieties of the postcolonial Canadian identity."[40] Lines in the novel like, "There's a kind of nice simplicity about a Canadian that education abroad seems to destroy,"[41] underline these sorts of questions of identity via the larger issue that the novel explores of restaging the colonial presence in Canada by way of Shakespeare. Identity, too, plays a key role in Davies's 1942 book *Shakespeare for Young Players*, an introductory course to Shakespeare specifically targeting youth. The section addressed "To the Pupil" begins by asking: "Are you an interesting person? . . . If you think about it for a little while you will see what an important question this is. We do not want to be dull, either to ourselves or to other people. We want to be interesting; we want to be liked."[42] The section concludes with Davies opining, "if you are not enjoying Shakespeare, you must be doing your work in a dull, uninteresting way."[43] The comments resonate within larger contexts that link identity and personal character to Shakespeare as a source for truths about the human condition that make Canadian youth, if they properly learn these, more interesting, more worthy.

This sort of high-mindedness is spoofed in *Tempest-Tost* with Davies, for instance, suggesting via the character of Mrs. Leakey that not only are Shakespeare's characters "awfully overdrawn," but that "it seems to me that more people would like Shakespeare if he had written in prose."[44] Another character in the novel, Hector, describes his "first encounter with *The Tempest*" as being like "the man who bites a peach and breaks a tooth upon the stone."[45] Such comments

---

39   Robertson Davies, *Tempest-Tost* (Toronto: Penguin, 2006), 233.
40   Kate O'Neill, "Re-writing the Colonial Experience: Robertson Davies' Use of Parody in *Tempest-Tost*," in *Rewriting Texts Remaking Images: Interdisciplinary Perspectives*, ed. Leslie Anne Boldt-Irons, Corrado Federici, and Ernesto Virgulti (New York: Peter Lang, 2010), 122.
41   Davies, *Tempest-Tost*, 28.
42   Robertson Davies, *Shakespeare for Young Players* (Toronto: Clarke, Irwin, 1942), ix.
43   Ibid., xi.
44   Davies, *Tempest-Tost*, 153.
45   Ibid., 46.

continue to reveal ways in which Canadians' cultural imaginary constructs itself via Shakespeare. In a strange twist, a theatrical adaptation of Davies's *Tempest-Tost* was performed in 2001 at the Stratford Festival (directed by Richard Rose), an unusual situation in which the original play prompted a novel, which in turn prompts the novel being turned into a play depicting the novel. No fear of refashioning here: in fact this form of meta-production points to how refashioning Shakespeare in a particular national context can also be aligned with conventional literary (that of Davies, one of Canada's most iconic writers) and theatrical histories (the Stratford Festival, perhaps Canada's most iconic arts institution, founded on its relation to Shakespeare).

The Davies example is hardly the only such prose version of the play in Canada. Mark Fortier's discussion of Winnipeg children's author Carol Matas and her 1999 novel *Cloning Miranda* points to how the novel has "significant echoes" with its source, including the "themes of technology, power, and ethics, nature and nurture, the dutiful daughter, and the monster."[46] None of these echoes are particularly Canadian. Yet, Fortier's insight that "to engage with Shakespeare is always to engage with some limitation of Shakespeare"[47] reminds us that attempts to circumscribe the potential meanings of Shakespeare will always be exceeded by the range of forms that the productions and adaptations can take—a practice abundantly in evidence in the Canadian versions of the play discussed here. A last set of examples of these sorts of adaptations drawn from very different genres will suffice to demonstrate how diverse these reimaginings can be.

Montreal-based director and actor Madd Harold, who has written *An Actor's Guide to Performing Shakespeare*, adapted and directed a queer version of *The Tempest: Forecast Disorder* in 2001 by Gravy Bath Productions, with an entirely male cast. The latter decision provocatively subverted the romantic clichés associated with the Ferdinand and Miranda relationship. That the production was set in an insane asylum further heightened how illusion and delusion are key elements in the source text. Earlier in 1988, French-Canadian director Alice Ronfard produced a radical intermedial adaptation of *La Tempête* using video screens at Espace GO, an important Montreal theatre space. The production featured women in all the male roles of the play, a not-so-subtle reminder of the androcentric world Shakespeare portrays on the island. The world-renowned circus company Cirque du Soleil, based out of Montreal and founded in 1984

46    Mark Fortier, "Undead and Unsafe: Adapting Shakespeare (in Canada)," in "*A World Elsewhere?*": *Shakespeare in Canada*, ed. Diana Brydon and Irena R. Makaryk (Toronto: University of Toronto Press, 2002), 346.
47    Ibid., 347.

by two Québécois street performers, Guy Laliberté and Gilles Ste-Croix, staged *Amaluna* in 2012, a very loose adaptation of *The Tempest* featuring another example of gender play. Prospero is now the shamanistic woman ruler Prospera, who governs an island of goddesses on which a shipwreck occurs. Miranda's love interest is Romeo, and the island is populated by multiple female presences including the Peacock Goddess, the Moon Goddess, the Balance Goddess, the Valkyries, and even Amazons. Large-scale touring productions like *Amaluna* reach significant numbers of people and generate significant economies—in 2012 the Cirque du Soleil generated over a billion dollars in revenue. Moreover, these sorts of productions, when digitally reproduced or disseminated via online or movie-style venues, can reach global audiences that might never think to link the origins of the production to its Canadian contexts.

This large-scale adaptation is to be contrasted with smaller productions and adaptations that are also very much the norm in Canada, with very focused, purposive directions arising from local circumstances, whether community or university theatre productions, or alternative and fringe productions, or more experimentalist genre-bending versions of the play. Karen Rickers's 2005 adaptation, *Tempest in a Teapot*, uses *The Tempest* to focus on slavery, liberation, and the effect of patriarchal expectation on the freedom of daughters. Director Michael Kelly's Shakespeare in Action (SIA) Company has explicit literacy-based and community-facing outcomes it associates with Shakespearean productions. Describing itself as "a multi-racial theatre company that aspires to enhance the arts and education through exploring and performing Shakespeare's plays," Shakespeare in Action presents "Canadian interpretations of Shakespeare and other classical and contemporary stories that are relevant to young audiences and their families and the community."[48] A 2013 production of *The Tempest* focused on blending first-time performers with experienced actors on the historic stage of the Central Commerce Theatre in Central Commerce Collegiate, downtown Toronto, which hosts one of the most ethnically diverse student bodies anywhere in Canada. The 2011 adaptation by west-coast Canadian choreographer Crystal Pite's contemporary dance company, Kidd Pivot, entitled *The Tempest Replica*, deploys motifs from the play pantomimed in marionette-like movements and by outfitting all the characters, save for Prospero, in faceless white masks and dressing them in white in the first half of the performance. The production replays two versions of the play: the first part on the island with Prospero in full control, orchestrating the faceless, masked dancers, and the second part with the dancers reclaiming their human identities in an urban setting and resisting Prospero's

---

48   Shakespeare in Action, "Company Mandate," accessed April 14, 2013, http://www.shakespeareinaction.org/company-history.

domination. Again, familiar issues of identity and control are front and centre in Pite's adaptation.

In addition to these examples from very different performance contexts, a range of translated versions of *The Tempest* have been created in French Canada, including Michel Garneau's previously mentioned 1973 translation (used by Robert Lepage), famed Acadian author Antonine Maillet's 1998 translation, and Normand Chaurette's version from the same year. Chaurette, a prominent Québécois playwright, author, and translator, has translated some dozen Shakespeare plays into French and has also authored a Governor General's Literary Award non-fiction book recounting his encounters with Shakespeare, *Comment tuer Shakespeare* (How to kill Shakespeare). The literary memoir chronicles his struggles with the iconic importance of Shakespeare and the need to remake his texts in ways that reflect on one's own cultural identity and formation. Chaurette's reflections on translating *The Tempest* arise from the question he asks himself: "And me, how often have I asked myself, how has Shakespeare killed me?"[49] The answer to the question surprisingly lies in *The Tempest*, what Chaurette calls Shakespeare's most perverse play, a play he has twice translated, yet a play he dislikes ("je n'aime pas cette pièce"[50]). The key to this dislike is Prospero, who Chaurette sees as a villain akin to *Othello*'s Iago: a seducer, someone who passes as a benefactor and a bogus model of philosophical kindness, largely thanks to the two monologues he speaks at the play's end.[51] Chaurette characterizes Prospero by saying:

> So here: the most detestable of fathers, the most off-putting of masters, the most sadistic of torturers, and the greatest usurper of kings, who on top of all this plays the role of usurped, here he is mysteriously absolved of the abyss by the contractor—and architect of hell [that is, by Shakespeare].[52]

In Chaurette's critically astute, visceral unmasking of Prospero's benevolence, the deceptive politics of his power plays, and his self-serving strategies, we find a radical take on the play—one that attacks patronizing notions of the benevolent

---

49   "Et moi, me suis-je si souvent demandé, comment Shakespeare m'avait-il tué?" Normand Chaurette, *Comment tuer Shakespeare* (Montréal: Les Presses de l'Université de Montréal, 2011), 206.

50   Ibid., 207.

51   Ibid., 206–207.

52   "Voilà: le plus détestable des pères, le plus rébarbatif des maîtres, le plus sadique des bourreaux, et le plus usurpateur des rois, qui joue l'usurpé par-dessus le marché, le voilà mystérieusement absout par le maître d'œuvre de l'abîme, et architecte de l'enfer" (my translation). Ibid., 207.

master, a familiar trope in English–French relations in Canada, and a familiar part of any form of critical discourse that addresses colonial and imperial relations. The insight reverses traditional interpretations and asks that we reconsider the machinations of *all* structures of power when they are aligned with forms of self-interest that make others suffer. This is how Shakespeare figuratively "kills" Chaurette, but it is also how Shakespeare is given new life in the critical contexts out of which Chaurette writes. Prospero's struggle occurs *within* imperial culture and he deploys colonial strategies to regain power, *not* to critique colonialism. To say this is to understand, as Paul Leonard argues, that the "conventional view of *The Tempest* as a gentle paean to reconciliation and renewal only makes sense once we acknowledge that the play requires everyone, characters and audience, to be reconciled to Prospero's dominance."[53]

Prospero is often read as the emblem of Shakespeare, the consummate theatrical magician who has mastered the technology of books, rhetoric, imagination, stagecraft, and illusion. His end and the breaking of his staff symbolize, in this reading, Shakespeare's public end, his symbolic death, his renunciation of what he has become. The move is infinitely ambiguous and open-ended, manipulative even, for it implies a form of destruction that releases renewed creative energies to which one is then forever tied. Death becomes immortality in the deepest sense of the endlessness of creative reinvention that depends on a kind of metaphorical destruction of what already is. Chaurette's clever reading of Shakespeare, which simultaneously invokes the killing of Shakespeare but also the killing of Chaurette by Shakespeare, merely restages and underlines this curious logic. Shakespeare rewritten in this intensely symbolic context becomes the architect of his own demise, a manipulator who, in Chaurette's reading, must be seen for what he truly is, and who is infinitely capable of being reborn and refashioned by this act of seeing. Here again, as I have argued elsewhere, "Shakespeare serves multiple identity formations, with differing consequences for how nation is constructed in relation to differing theatrical discourses."[54] *The Tempest*, then, provides a unique crucible for understanding some of these permutations in relation to contested notions of what Canada means, making the answer to the question "where is here?" always, inconclusively and contingently, *here*—in these words, in these acts and scenes.

---

53   Leonard, "*The Tempest* x 2," 12.
54   Daniel Fischlin, "Nation and/as Adaptation: Shakespeare, Canada, and Authenticity," in "*A World Elsewhere?*": *Shakespeare in Canada*, ed. Diana Brydon and Irena R. Makaryk (Toronto: University of Toronto Press, 2002), 313.

# Works Cited

Atwood, Margaret. *Survival: A Thematic Guide to Canadian Literature*. Toronto: House of Anansi Press, 2013.

Bennett, Susan. "The Post-colonial Body? Thinking Through *The Tempest*." In *Performing Nostalgia: Shifting Shakespeare and the Contemporary Past*, 119–50. London: Routledge, 1996.

Chaurette, Normand. *Comment tuer Shakespeare*. Montréal: Les Presses de l'Université de Montréal, 2011.

Davies, Robertson. *Shakespeare for Young Players*. Toronto: Clarke, Irwin, 1942.

———. *Tempest-Tost*. Toronto: Penguin, 2006.

Fischlin, Daniel. "David Garneau." In "Shakespeare in Canadian Art." *Canadian Adaptations of Shakespeare Project*. Accessed April 14, 2013, http://www.canadianshakespeares.ca/multimedia/imagegallery/m_i_2.cfm.

———. "Nation and/as Adaptation: Shakespeare, Canada, and Authenticity." In "*A World Elsewhere?*": *Shakespeare in Canada*, edited by Diana Brydon and Irena R. Makaryk, 313–38. Toronto: University of Toronto Press, 2002.

———. "The Tempest." *Canadian Adaptations of Shakespeare Project. Accessed April 14, 2013,* http://www.canadianshakespeares.ca/Production_Shakespeare/SearchPublicShowPlay.cfm?PlayID=651.

Fortier, Mark. "'In no recognizable way' *The Tempest*." In *Negation, Critical Theory, and Postmodern Textuality*, edited by Daniel Fischlin, 59–87. Dordrecht: Kluwer, 1994.

———. "Undead and Unsafe: Adapting Shakespeare (in Canada)." In "*A World Elsewhere?*": *Shakespeare in Canada*, edited by Diana Brydon and Irena R. Makaryk, 339–52 Toronto: University of Toronto Press, 2002.

Frye, Northrop. "Conclusion to the First Edition of *Literary History of Canada*." In *Northrop Frye on Canada*, edited by Jean O'Grady and David Staines. Vol. 12 of *The Collected Works of Northrop Frye*, 339–72. Toronto: University of Toronto Press, [1965] 2003.

———. "Foreword to *The Prospect of Change*." In *Northrop Frye on Canada*, edited by Jean O'Grady and David Staines. Vol. 12 of *The Collected Works of Northrop Frye*, 373–76. Toronto: University of Toronto Press, [1965] 2003.

———. "Introduction to Shakespeare's *Tempest*." In *Northrop Frye's Writings on Shakespeare and the Renaissance*, edited by Troni Y. Grande and Garry Sherbert. Vol. 28 of *The Collected Works of Northrop Frye*, 44–52. Toronto: University of Toronto Press, [1959] 2010.

——. *The Myth of Deliverance: Reflections on Shakespeare's Problem Comedies.* Toronto: University of Toronto Press, 1983.

——. "Preface to *The Bush Garden.*" In *Northrop Frye on Canada*, edited by Jean O'Grady and David Staines. Vol. 12 of *The Collected Works of Northrop Frye*, 412–20. Toronto: University of Toronto Press, [1971] 2003.

"*La Tempête*, Directed by Robert Lepage in July 2011." Ex Machina press release. 2011.

Leonard, Paul. "*The Tempest* x 2 in Toronto." *Canadian Theatre Review* 54, no.4 (1988): 7–12.

Makaryk, Irena R. "Canada." In *The Oxford Companion to Shakespeare*, edited by Michael Dobson and Stanley Wells, 64–65. Oxford: Oxford University Press, 2001.

——. "'Wider Still and Wider': Societies and Universities." In "Shakespeare in Canada: 'A World Elsewhere'?" *The Internet Shakespeare.* Accessed April 12, 2013, http://internet-shakespeare.uvic.ca/Library/Criticism/shakespearein/canada4.html.

Montaigne, Michel Eyquem de. "Of the Caniballes." *The Essays of Montaigne's Done into English by John Florio*, vol. 1, 217–32. London: David Nutt by the Strand, [1603] 1892.

Miller, Shannon. *Invested With Meaning: The Raleigh Circle in the New World.* Philadelphia, PA: University of Pennyslvania Press, 1998.

O'Neill, Kate. "Re-writing the Colonial Experience: Robertson Davies' Use of Parody in *Tempest-Tost.*" In *Rewriting Texts Remaking Images: Interdisciplinary Perspectives*, edited by Leslie Anne Boldt-Irons, Corrado Federici, and Ernesto Virgulti, 121–32. New York: Peter Lang, 2010.

Shakespeare in Action. "Company Mandate." Accessed April 14, 2013, http://www.shake-speareinaction.org/company-history.

Stevenson, Orlando John. *Shakespeare's* The Tempest. *With annotations by O.J. Stevenson.* Toronto: Copp Clark, 1927.

Windspeaker, Marie White. "Huron-Wendat Village of Wendake Stage *The Tempest.*" *AMMSA* 29, no. 6 (2011). Accessed May 30, 2013, http://www.ammsa.com/publications/windspeaker/huron-wendat-village-wendake-stages-tempest.

Wilson, Sir Daniel. *Caliban: The Missing Link.* London: Macmillan and Co., 1873.

Yachnin, Paul. "*The Tempest*: Critical Introduction." *The Internet Shakespeare.* Accessed April 12, 2013, http://internetshakespeare.uvic.ca/Annex/Texts/Tmp/intro/GenIntro/default/.

# Character Synopses

### ALONSO, King of Naples

ALONSO is the King of Naples who, along with most of the rest of the characters, is returning from the wedding of his daughter, Claribel, in Algiers. He is the father of FERDINAND, from whom he is separated during the apparent sinking of the ship at the beginning of the play. Despondent at his loss, he is inconsolable through much of the play. Years prior, when PROSPERO was the Duke of Milan, ALONSO was at least partially complicit in the plot to remove PROSPERO from power.

### SEBASTIAN, his brother

SEBASTIAN is the younger brother of ALONSO who, along with ANTONIO, conspires to usurp the throne of Naples while they are shipwrecked. He describes himself as incredibly lazy and needs to be goaded into acting against his brother by ANTONIO.

### PROSPERO, the rightful Duke of Milan

PROSPERO is a magus (a scholar of the magical arts) as well as the rightful Duke of Milan. Years earlier, he was deposed by his brother, ANTONIO, who ordered that he be set adrift with his daughter, MIRANDA. Landing on the island, he discovers CALIBAN and ARIEL. As the play opens, PROSPERO seizes his opportunity to reclaim the dukedom and show mercy to his traitorous brother.

### MIRANDA, daughter to PROSPERO

MIRANDA is the daughter of PROSPERO. She has vague memories of her time as a princess in Milan, yet has been essentially brought up on the island with CALIBAN. Years prior, CALIBAN attempted to sexually assault MIRANDA. She eventually becomes engaged to FERDINAND.

### ANTONIO, the usurping Duke of Milan, brother to PROSPERO

ANTONIO is the Duke of Milan in name only, after having unwittingly exiled his brother, PROSPERO, to the island, thinking that he had killed him. He convinces SEBASTIAN to kill ALONSO and take the crown of Naples. Eventually, he is brought under the power of PROSPERO, who chooses to show mercy and forgive him.

### FERDINAND, son to the King of Naples

FERDINAND is the son of ALONSO, who thinks he is dead following the apparent shipwreck at the beginning of the play. Upon meeting MIRANDA, by modern standards, he is inordinately interested in finding out if she is a virgin or not, yet this can be read as both awkwardness and a part of the early modern obsession with the trustworthiness of female bodies. He eventually becomes engaged to MIRANDA after being tested by PROSPERO to determine the strength of his love for her. The first thing he does upon their engagement is to cheat while playing a game of chess with her.

### GONZALO, an honest old counsellor

GONZALO was a minister to PROSPERO when he was the Duke of Milan and, though told to assassinate PROSPERO and MIRANDA by ANTONIO, he instead puts them on a boat at sea with provisions and books. At the opening of the play, he is the chief minister of ALONSO and spends most of the play trying to bring him out of his depression following the apparent death of FERDINAND.

### CALIBAN, a savage and deformed slave

The only son of Sycorax, a witch from Algiers who was banished to the island and died some years before, CALIBAN was raised by PROSPERO with MIRANDA. PROSPERO governs CALIBAN using magical bodily punishments. CALIBAN attempts to get TRINCULO and STEPHANO to kill PROSPERO and take over the island. His name probably comes from the same root as "cannibal" and "Caribbean." CALIBAN, unlike TRINCULO and STEPHANO, speaks predominantly in verse.

### ARIEL, an airy spirit

Years before, ARIEL was a servant of the witch Sycorax, who imprisoned him for refusing to do her bidding. He was released by PROSPERO, who puts him to use as his chief spirit and executor of his commands. ARIEL has the ability to shape-shift and to control the elements. He serves PROSPERO as an indentured servant who is also given control over other spirits during the play, and his promised release at the end of the play is used by PROSPERO as a motivator throughout.

### TRINCULO, a jester

TRINCULO is a well-travelled jester at the court of ALONSO who joins with CALIBAN and STEPHANO to try to kill PROSPERO.

### STEPHANO, a drunken butler

STEPHANO is the butler of ALONSO and washes ashore with a cask of wine, which he drinks with CALIBAN and TRINCULO. Together the trio plots to kill PROSPERO.

### MASTER of a ship

The master of the ship appears only briefly in act one to order the Boatswain to govern the mariners.

### BOATSWAIN

The BOATSWAIN is the foreman of the deck crew. In many editions, this is abbreviated to "Bos'n," which is closer to how it is pronounced.

### Mariners

The sailors on the ship at the beginning of the play.

### IRIS

Messenger goddess whose symbol is the rainbow. Appears onstage to bless the wedding of MIRANDA and FERDINAND. Whether it is actually the goddess or a spirit under the guidance of ARIEL pretending to be IRIS is not completely clear.

### CERES

Goddess of the harvest. Appears on stage to bless the wedding of MIRANDA and FERDINAND. Whether it is actually the goddess or a spirit under the guidance of ARIEL pretending to be CERES is not completely clear.

### JUNO

Queen of the gods. Appears on stage to bless the wedding of MIRANDA and FERDINAND. Whether it is actually the goddess or a spirit under the guidance of ARIEL pretending to be JUNO is not completely clear.

## Nymphs

Appear as a part of the masque of celebration in honour of the wedding of MIRANDA and FERDINAND.

## Reapers

Appear as a part of the masque of celebration in honour of the wedding of MIRANDA and FERDINAND.

## Spirits

Personifications of elemental forces working under the guidance of ARIEL.

# THE TEMPEST

Note on the synopsis: More than any other play he wrote, Shakespeare built this work around the five-act structure, inherited from a Roman (mis)interpretation of ancient Greek theatrical practice. The play's final two acts are each one scene long, while the first act is, in essence, a single scene with a dramatic introduction. Acts two and three are broken up across the three subplots (the young lovers, FERDINAND and MIRANDA; the court following ALONSO; and the trio of conspirators, CALIBAN, STEPHANO, and TRINCULO), yet these acts are comparatively clean in terms of their structure and pacing. This adherence to the acts over scenes as the dominant organizational principle is why this edition has chosen not to provide a synopsis of each act in addition to a synopsis of each scene. In acts four and five it would be superfluous, while in act three it would obscure the clarity of differentiation of the subplots in each scene.

# ACT ONE, SCENE ONE (1.1)

The play begins in the middle of things (a device technically known by its Latin name, *in medias res*). The scene is a dramatic opening to the play, introducing the questions of authority and governance that run throughout the text.

A massive storm batters a ship at sea that is carrying the court of the King of Naples, ALONSO. The ship's MASTER orders the BOATSWAIN to organize the mariners against the storm, yet the nobles of the court, especially GONZALO, get in the way throughout the first scene. GONZALO suggests that the BOATSWAIN looks as though he was born to be hanged rather than drowned at sea, while the other nobles—notably ANTONIO and SEBASTIAN—deride and insult the mariners. Eventually, it appears as though the ship is splitting in two and ready to sink.

**Act One**
**Scene One**

*A tempestuous noise of thunder and lightning heard.*[1] *Enter a SHIPMASTER*[2] *and a BOATSWAIN.*[3]

**Master** Boatswain!
**Boatswain** Here, Master. What cheer?
**Master** Good,[4] speak to the Mariners. Fall to't, yarely,[5] or we run ourselves aground. Bestir, bestir![6]

*[Exit.]*

*Enter MARINERS.*

**Boatswain** Hey, my hearts! Cheerly, cheerly, my hearts! Yare, yare! Take in the 5
topsail. Tend to the master's whistle. Blow till thou burst thy wind, if room enough!

---

1    A tempestuous . . . heard  Among Shakespeare's plays, *The Tempest* is unique for having the fullest and most descriptive stage directions. Whereas many of his plays simply note entrances and exits of characters, *The Tempest* dictates many elements of presentation, including, here, the tempest itself.
2    SHIP*MASTER*  Hereafter, simply "MASTER."
3.   BOATSWAIN  A boatswain is the foreman of the deck crew. In many editions, this is abbreviated to "Bos'n," which is closer to how it is pronounced.
4    *Good*  Not "good cheer" but an expression of delight at the presence of the boatswain.
5    *yarely*  Briskly.
6    *bestir*  Arise, act quickly, rouse oneself.

*Enter ALONSO, SEBASTIAN, ANTONIO, FERDINAND, GONZALO,*
*and others.*

***Alonzo*** Good Boatswain, have care. Where's the Master? [*To the MARINERS.*]
Play the men.[7]

***Boatswain*** I pray now, keep below.                                                            10

***Alonzo*** Where is the Master, Boatswain?

***Boatswain*** Do you not hear him? You mar our labour. Keep your cabins; you
do assist the storm.

***Gonzalo*** Nay, good,[8] be patient.

***Boatswain*** When the sea is. Hence! What cares these roarers[9] for the name of     15
king? To cabin—silence! Trouble us not.

***Gonzalo*** Good, yet remember whom thou hast aboard.

***Boatswain*** None that I more love than myself. You are a counsellor—if you can
command these elements to silence, and work the peace of the present, we
will not hand[10] a rope more—use your authority. If you cannot, give thanks     20
you have lived so long, and make yourself ready in your cabin for the
mischance of the hour, if it so hap. [*To the MARINERS.*] Cheerly, good
hearts! [*To the courtiers.*] Out of our way, I say.

[*Exit.*]

***Gonzalo*** I have great comfort from this fellow. Methinks he hath no drowning
mark upon him—his complexion is perfect gallows.[11] Stand fast, good Fate,     25
to his hanging. Make the rope of his destiny our cable, for our own doth
little advantage. If he be not born to be hanged, our case is miserable.

[*Exeunt.*[12]]

*Enter BOATSWAIN.*

---

7    *Play the men*  Act like men.
8    *good*  "Good man," as opposed to the earlier use.
9    *roarers*  Waves, with a double meaning of the mariners.
10   hand  Handle.
11   *his complexion . . . gallows*  Proverbial—"he that was born to be hanged shall never be
      drowned." R.W. Dent, *Shakespeare's Proverbial Language: An Index* (Berkeley, CA: University
      of California Press, 1981), B139.
12   Exeunt  A Latin term meaning "exit," used when multiple people leave the stage. "*Exeunt
      omnes*" means "Exit all."

**Boatswain** Down with the topmast![13] Yare! Lower, lower! Bring her to try with main-course.[14] A plague—

*A cry within.*

*Enter SEBASTIAN, ANTONIO, and GONZALO.*

—upon this howling! They are louder than the weather or our office. Yet again! What do you here? Shall we give o'er and drown? Have you a mind to sink?                                                                                                30

**Sebastian** A pox o' your throat, you bawling, blasphemous, incharitable dog!

**Boatswain** Work you, then.

**Antonio** Hang, cur,[15] hang, you whoreson, insolent noisemaker! We are less afraid to be drowned than thou art.                                                          35

**Gonzalo** I'll warrant him[16] for drowning; though the ship were no stronger than a nutshell and as leaky as an unstanched wench.[17]

**Boatswain** Lay her a-hold, a-hold![18] Set her two courses[19] off to sea again; lay her off![20]                                                                                            40

*Enter MARINERS wet.*

**Mariners** All lost! To prayers, to prayers! All lost!

**Boatswain** What, must our mouths be cold?[21]

---

13  *Topmast* The second section of a square-rigged sailing ship's mast, immediately above the lower mast. The topmast is lowered to bring the centre of gravity down and prevent the ship from moving towards the shore.

14  *main-course* The main sail. The implication is that the mariners should keep the ship away from the island and move it to open sea. The phrase used with this specific nautical meaning appears in Captain John Smith's *Sea Grammar* (1627) and *Accidence for Young Sea-men* (1626) as well as in Hakluyt's *Voyages* (1598), as described by H.H. Furness, *The Tempest: New Variorum Edition* (Philadelphia: J.B. Lippincott Co., 1892), 17.

15  *cur* An aggressive dog. Also, a contemptible man.

16  *warrant him* Guarantee him against.

17  *Unstanched wench* Multiple meanings are available here. "Stanch" and "stench" were homonyms in the period, lending an olfactory reading, though the primary reading would be referencing the supposed "leakiness" of the female body. A "stanch" was "that which stops or allays" (*Oxford English Dictionary*, 3rd ed., s.v. "stanch," n1), usually fluids and particularly blood (ibid., n2). Thus, an unstanched woman could be a woman in her menstrual cycle, or a derogatory reference to post-coital flow, both of which were held to be dangerous to men in early modern medical discourse. Further, there is the possibility of a homonymic relationship with "staunch," suggesting an "unstaunch" or disloyal woman; a prostitute. One should not think that there is one meaning or even one preferred meaning to Shakespeare's words. They had no dictionaries in Shakespeare's day and relied wholly on auditory memory, making London a melting pot of different cultures, languages, and possible linguistic references.

18  *lay a-hold* Set the ship close to the wind.

19  *courses* Sails.

20  *lay her off* Set the ship away from shore.

21  *mouths be cold* To be cold in the mouth was proverbial for death, though some performances have the boatswain take a swig of a flask at this point.

**Gonzalo**  The king and prince at prayers! Let's assist them,
  For our case is as theirs.
**Sebastian**                              I'm out of patience.
**Antonio**  We are merely cheated of our lives by drunkards:                45
  This wide-chapped rascal—would thou might'st lie drowning
  The washing of ten tides![22]
**Gonzalo**                              He'll be hanged yet,
  Though every drop of water swear against it
  And gape at widest to glut him.

  *A confused noise within.*

  "Mercy on us!"—"We split, we split!"—"Farewell, my wife and children!"—   50
  "Farewell, brother!"—"We split, we split, we split!"
**Antonio**  Let's all sink with the king.
**Sebastian**  Let's take leave of him.

                    *Exeunt [ANTONIO and SEBASTIAN.]*

**Gonzalo**  Now would I give a thousand furlongs of sea for an acre of barren
  ground—long heath, brown furze,[23] anything. The wills above be done, but    55
  I would fain die a dry death.

                                        *[Exeunt.]*


# ACT ONE, SCENE TWO (1.2)

The next scene takes place on the island of PROSPERO, where MIRANDA has witnessed the apparent sinking of the ship. She asks her father to end the storm, if it was his magic that raised it. Eventually, PROSPERO tells her that it is time to reveal to her the secret of her past and why it is that they are on the island. He tells her that a long time ago he was the Duke of Milan, during which time he focused all of his attentions on studying and learning the magical arts and gave his brother, ANTONIO, the governance of the city. ANTONIO, however, was not content to rule in deed rather than in name and conspired with the King of Naples, ALONSO, to usurp PROSPERO and kill both him and his young daughter. Rather than killing him outright, ANTONIO ordered that PROSPERO be set adrift at sea, but the minister who was put in charge of the

---

22   *ten tides*  Pirates, when caught, were hanged on shore for at least three tides.
23   *long heath, brown furze*  Heather and gorse. These plants grow in poor soil.

assassination, GONZALO, provided PROSPERO with his magic books and provisions. Eventually washing ashore on the island, they eked out a life together.

After relating the story of their past to MIRANDA, PROSPERO casts a spell to put her to sleep and calls on his servant, ARIEL, with whom he talks about the apparent sinking of the ship. ARIEL eventually asks when he will be set free by PROSPERO, who becomes angry. ARIEL was the servant of Sycorax, the mother of CALIBAN, in the years before PROSPERO came to the island. He would not do her magical bidding and, for that, she imprisoned him in a pine. PROSPERO released him and for that, ARIEL has served him ever since. PROSPERO sends ARIEL to appear as a sea nymph and MIRANDA awakes.

Upon her awakening, PROSPERO suggests that they visit CALIBAN. CALIBAN at first refuses to see the pair, yet upon PROSPERO's threats, he emerges. PROSPERO claims that he tried to raise CALIBAN with MIRANDA like a brother, until CALIBAN attempted to sexually assault her. After that incident, he confined CALIBAN to a rock and has since used him as a slave. PROSPERO then orders CALIBAN to fetch firewood and as he leaves, ARIEL returns, singing and leading FERDINAND, the son of the King of Naples, onto the stage.

FERDINAND and MIRANDA see each other and are instantly attracted to one another. To make the courtship more meaningful to both of them, PROSPERO tries to convince MIRANDA that FERDINAND is ugly and her ignorance can't detect the difference. Then, PROSPERO takes FERDINAND in as a prisoner and leads them all offstage.

## Act One
## Scene Two

*Enter PROSPERO and MIRANDA.*

**Miranda**  If by your art,[24] my dearest father, you have
Put the wild waters in this roar, allay them.[25]
The sky, it seems, would pour down stinking pitch,[26]
But that the sea, mounting to th' welkin's cheek,[27]
Dashes the fire out. O, I have suffered                    5

---

24  *art*  Magic. Prospero's hermetic magic is repeatedly contrasted with the black arts of Sycorax throughout this scene.
25  *allay them*  Calm them.
26  *stinking pitch*  Miranda suggests that the clouds are so black that they may produce tar.
27  *welkin's cheek*  The "welkin" was another name for the sky, so a cheek would be a cloud.

With those that I saw suffer. A brave[28] vessel—
Who had, no doubt, some noble creature in her—
Dashed all to pieces! O, the cry did knock
Against my very heart. Poor souls, they perished.
Had I been any god of power, I would                                          10
Have sunk the sea within the earth or ere
It should the good ship so have swallowed, and
The fraughting[29] souls within her.

**Prospero**                                    Be collected;[30]
No more amazement.[31] Tell your piteous heart
There's no harm done.

**Miranda**                           O, woe the day!

**Prospero**                                    No harm.                       15
I have done nothing but in care of thee,
Of thee, my dear one, thee, my daughter, who
Art ignorant of what thou art; naught knowing
Of whence I am,[32] nor that I am more better[33]
Than Prospero, master of a full poor cell,                                    20
And thy no greater father.

**Miranda**                           More to know
Did never meddle[34] with my thoughts.[35]

**Prospero**                                    'Tis time
I should inform thee farther. Lend thy hand,
And pluck my magic garment from me. So:

[*Disrobes with MIRANDA's help.*]

Lie there, my art.[36]—Wipe thou thine eyes; have comfort.                    25
The direful spectacle of the wreck, which touched
The very virtue of compassion[37] in thee,

---

28   *brave*   Fine or excellent.
29   *fraughting*   That which forms freight or cargo, though there is wordplay here. A fraught soul is
     a soul that is overburdened (with guilt), such as Alonso's or Antonio's.
30   *Be collected*   Compose yourself.
31   *amazement*   Worry, though also to be brought into a state of confusion and wonder as
     though lost in a maze.
32   *whence I am*   Where I am from.
33   *more better*   More distinguished.
34   *meddle*   Mix into.
35   *More to . . . thoughts*   Is Miranda playing into her father's image of her as merely an innocent,
     or is she so isolated and unaware that she honestly had never thought of learning more about
     her own history?
36   *Lie there, my art*   Prospero's magic robe, like his books and his staff, is an embodiment of his
     learning.
37   *virtue of compassion*   Essence of compassion, but also that compassion was a virtue.

I have with such provision in mine art
So safely ordered that there is no soul,
No, not so much perdition as an hair                              30
Betid³⁸ to any creature in the vessel
Which thou heard'st cry, which thou saw'st sink. Sit down;
For thou must now know farther.
*Miranda*                              You have often
Begun to tell me what I am, but stopped
And left me to a bootless inquisition,³⁹                          35
Concluding, "Stay, not yet."
*Prospero*                              The hour's now come;
The very minute bids thee ope thine ear.⁴⁰
Obey, and be attentive. Canst thou remember
A time before we came unto this cell?
I do not think thou canst, for then thou wast⁴¹ not            40
Out⁴² three years old.
*Miranda*                              Certainly, sir, I can.
*Prospero*  By what? By any other house or person?⁴³
Of anything the image tell me that
Hath kept with thy remembrance.⁴⁴
*Miranda*                              'Tis far off
And rather like a dream than an assurance                       45
That my remembrance warrants.⁴⁵ Had I not
Four or five women once that tended⁴⁶ me?
*Prospero*  Thou hadst, and more, Miranda; but how is it
That this lives in thy mind? What see'st thou else
In the dark backward and abysm⁴⁷ of time?                       50
If thou rememb'rest aught ere thou cam'st here,
How thou cam'st here thou mayst.
*Miranda*                              But that I do not.

---

**Prospero**  Twelve year since, Miranda, twelve year since,
    Thy father was the Duke of Milan[48] and
    A prince of power—
**Miranda**                 Sir, are not you my father?        55
**Prospero**  Thy mother was a piece[49] of virtue, and
    She said thou wast my daughter; and thy father
    Was Duke of Milan; and thou his only heir
    And princess, no worse issued.[50]
**Miranda**                   O, the heavens!
    What foul play had we that we came from thence?        60
    Or blessed was't we did?
**Prospero**             Both, both, my girl.
    By foul play, as thou sayst, were we heaved thence,
    But blessedly holp[51] hither.
**Miranda**               O, my heart bleeds
    To think o' th' teen that I have turned you to, [52]
    Which is from my remembrance. Please you, farther.    65
**Prospero**  My brother and thy uncle, called Antonio—
    I pray thee, mark me—that a brother should
    Be so perfidious—he whom next thyself
    Of all the world I loved and to him put
    The manage[53] of my state, as at that time    70
    Through all the signories[54] it was the first,
    And Prospero the prime duke, being so reputed
    In dignity, and for the liberal arts[55]
    Without a parallel; those being all my study,
    The government I cast upon my brother    75
    And to my state grew stranger, being transported
    And rapt in secret studies. Thy false uncle—
    Dost thou attend me?[56]

---

48   *Milan*  Pronounced in Shakespeare's England as "Mìlan," with the accent on the first syllable.
49   *piece*  Masterpiece.
50   *his only . . . issued*  Miranda's birth was no worse than that of a princess, though technically she is merely the daughter of a duke.
51   *holp*  Helped.
52   *To think . . . to*  "Teen" meant "trouble," thus, "To think of the trouble I caused you then."
53   *manage*  Governance.
54   *signories*  Governorships of an Italian state.
55   *the liberal arts*  Medieval universities taught the *trivium* (grammar, logic, rhetoric) and the *quadrivium* (arithmetic, geometry, music, astronomy), known as the liberal arts, while other schools taught professional disciplines like medicine, law, and so forth.
56   *my brother . . . me*  The elliptical syntax in this speech may indicate Prospero's emotional turmoil at retelling the story of his brother's betrayal.

**Miranda**                    Sir, most heedfully.
**Prospero**  Being once perfected[57] how to grant suits,
    How to deny them, who t' advance and who                    80
    To trash[58] for over-topping,[59] new created
    The creatures[60] that were mine, I say, or changed 'em,
    Or else new formed 'em; having both the key
    Of officer and office,[61] set all hearts i' th' state
    To what tune pleased his ear, that now he was                    85
    The ivy which had hid my princely trunk,
    And sucked my verdure out on't[62]—thou attend'st not.
**Miranda**  O, good sir, I do![63]
**Prospero**                    I pray thee, mark me:
    I, thus neglecting worldly ends, all dedicated
    To closeness[64] and the bettering of my mind                    90
    With that which, but by being so retired,
    O'er-prized all popular rate,[65] in my false brother
    Awaked an evil nature; and my trust,
    Like a good parent, did beget of him
    A falsehood in its contrary as great                    95
    As my trust was, which had, indeed, no limit,
    A confidence sans bound.[66] He being thus lorded,[67]
    Not only with what my revenue yielded,
    But what my power might else exact,[68] like one
    Who having into truth, by telling of it,                    100
    Made such a sinner of his memory,
    To credit his own lie, he did believe

---

57   *perfected*  Developed mastery in.
58   *trash*  Drawn from hunting discourse. To check (a hound) by keeping it on a leash.
59   *over-topping*  Taking on too much authority.
60   *creatures*  Dependants or clients.
61   *key . . . and office*  Governance of the administrators and the government.
62   *The ivy . . . on't*  The ivy (Antonio) covers the tree (Prospero), but (in this case) also sucks out the health, greenness, and vitality (verdure) from it.
63   *O, good . . . do*  Is Miranda genuinely not listening, or is Prospero so inattentive to his daughter that he can't tell that she is listening?
64   *closeness*  Seclusion, confinement, cloistering as in a monastery.
65   *With that . . . rate*  "With my studies, which were of greater value in my eyes than popularity—the only drawback being that they withdrew me from public life." O.J. Stevenson, *The Tempest* (Toronto: Copp Clark, 1927), 81.
66   *sans bound*  Without limit.
67   *lorded*  Made lord.
68   *But what . . . exact*  He increased the revenue of his office by forcing taxes upon the people.

He was indeed the duke,[69] out o' th' substitution[70]
And executing th' outward face of royalty,
With all prerogative.[71] Hence his ambition growing—                              105
Dost thou hear?
**Miranda**                  Your tale, sir, would cure deafness.
**Prospero**  To have no screen between this part he played
And him he played it for, he needs will be
Absolute Milan.[72] Me, poor man, my library
Was dukedom large enough. Of temporal royalties[73]                              110
He thinks me now incapable; confederates—
So dry[74] he was for sway—wi' th' King of Naples
To give him annual tribute, do him homage,[75]
Subject his coronet to his crown and bend
The dukedom yet unbowed—alas, poor Milan!—                              115
To most ignoble stooping.
**Miranda**                              O, the heavens!
**Prospero**  Mark his condition[76] and th' event, then tell me
If this might be a brother.
**Miranda**                              I should sin
To think but nobly of my grandmother,
Good wombs have borne bad sons.[77]
**Prospero**                              Now the condition.                              120
The King of Naples, being an enemy
To me inveterate, hearkens my brother's suit,
Which was, that he, in lieu o' th' premises[78]
Of homage and I know not how much tribute,

---

69  *like one . . . duke*  Like one who, having made his memory sin against (into) truth by lying so
     much, actually believes his own lie.
70  *out o' th' substitution*  By virtue of substitution.
71  *out of . . . prerogative*  He had served as my substitute and acted with all the powers of
     royalty.
72  *Absolute Milan*  The Duke of Milan.
73  *temporal royalties*  Secular authorities.
74  *dry*  Thirsty.
75  *homage*  Homage was a feudal custom tied up with vassalage. To do homage to a lord was
     to recognize that lord's power over you. Prospero refused to recognize Alonso's power over
     Milan, while Antonio did. This word introduces the discourse of feudal vassalage and con-
     tracted servitude prominent throughout the play.
76  *condition*  Terms of the contract with Naples.
77  *Good wombs . . . sons*  Proverbial. Many early modern proverbs dealt with the inherent
     untrustworthiness of female bodies.
78  *in lieu . . . premises*  In return for the conditions.

Should presently extirpate[79] me and mine                               125
Out of the dukedom and confer fair Milan,
With all the honours on my brother; whereon,
A treacherous army levied, one midnight
Fated[80] to the purpose did Antonio open
The gates of Milan, and, i' th' dead of darkness,                        130
The ministers for the purpose hurried thence
Me and thy crying self.

**Miranda**                        Alack, for pity!
I, not rememb'ring how I cried out then,
Will cry it o'er again. It is a hint[81]
That wrings mine eyes to't.[82]

**Prospero**                          Hear a little further,               135
And then I'll bring thee to the present business
Which now's upon's,[83] without the which this story
Were most impertinent.[84]

**Miranda**                        Wherefore[85] did they not
That hour destroy us?

**Prospero**                          Well demanded,[86] wench:[87]
My tale provokes that question. Dear, they durst[88] not,                 140
So dear the love my people bore me, nor set
A mark so bloody on the business;[89] but
With colours fairer painted their foul ends.
In few,[90] they hurried us aboard a barque,[91]
Bore us some leagues to sea, where they prepared                         145
A rotten carcass of a boat, not rigged,
Nor tackle, sail, nor mast—the very rats
Instinctively have quit it.[92] There they hoist us,

---

79   *presently extirpate*   Immediately to pull out by the roots.
80   *Fated*   Chosen by fate.
81   *hint*   Occasion.
82   *That wrings . . . to't*   Miranda is crying.
83   *upon's*   Upon us.
84   *impertinent*   Without reason; also, rude; also, not pertinent or germane.
85   *Wherefore*   Why.
86   *demanded*   Asked.
87   *wench*   Any young woman.
88   *durst*   Dared.
89   *mark so . . . business*   Any violence would have revealed their actions as treason.
90   *few*   Few words.
91   *barque*   A ship. That said, Milan is an inland city and has no port.
92   *have quit it*   Had abandoned it.

To cry to th' sea that roared to us, to sigh
To the winds whose pity, sighing back again,                    150
Did us but loving wrong.

**Miranda**                                        Alack, what trouble
Was I then to you!

**Prospero**                              O, a cherubim[93]
Thou wast that did preserve me. Thou did'st smile,
Infused with a fortitude from heaven,
When I have decked[94] the sea with drops full salt,            155
Under my burthen groaned, which[95] raised in me
An undergoing stomach[96] to bear up
Against what[97] should ensue.

**Miranda**                                        How came we ashore?

**Prospero**  By providence divine;
Some food we had, and some fresh water, that                    160
A noble Neapolitan, Gonzalo,
Out of his charity, being then appointed
Master of this design, did give us, with
Rich garments, linens, stuffs and necessaries,
Which since have steaded[98] much; so, of his gentleness,       165
Knowing I loved my books, he furnished me
From mine own library with volumes that
I prize above my dukedom.[99]

**Miranda**                                        Would I might
But ever see that man![100]

**Prospero**                              Now I arise.
Sit still, and hear the last[101] of our sea-sorrow:            170
Here in this island we arrived, and here
Have I, thy schoolmaster, made thee more profit

---

93  *cherubim* Diminutive form of cherub, a kind of angel often represented as a child with wings; also regarded in traditional Christian angelology as an angel of the second-highest order of the ninefold celestial hierarchy.
94  *decked* Covered.
95  *which* Miranda's smile.
96  *undergoing stomach* Endurance, courage. We still use "stomach" in this sense today—if someone has the "stomach" to do a difficult task.
97  *what* Whatever.
98  *steaded* Served our needs.
99  *I prize . . . dukedom* There is an intriguing tense shift here. Prospero's project is to retake Milan and, in doing so, give up his magical arts (literally, to drown his books), yet if that is so, why is he claiming here that he still prizes his books above his dukedom?
100  *Would I . . . man* I only wish I could someday see that man.
101  *last* Last part of the story.

Than other princesses can that have more time
For vainer hours, and tutors not so careful.[102]

**Miranda** Heavens thank you for't. And now, I pray you, sir,                    175
For still 'tis beating in my mind, your reason
For raising this sea-storm?

**Prospero**                    Know thus far forth.
By accident most strange, bountiful Fortune,
—Now my dear lady[103]—hath mine enemies
Brought to this shore, and by my prescience                    180
I find my zenith[104] doth depend upon
A most auspicious star, whose influence
If now I court not, but omit, my fortunes
Will ever after droop. Here cease more questions.
Thou art inclined to sleep. 'Tis a good dullness,[105]                    185
And give it way[106]—I know thou canst not choose.

[*MIRANDA sleeps.*]

Come away,[107] servant, come.

[*Puts on his magic cloak.*]

I am ready now.
Approach, my Ariel, come.

*Enter ARIEL.*

**Ariel** All hail, great master; grave sir, hail! I come                    190
To answer thy best pleasure, be't to fly,
To swim, to dive into the fire, to ride
On the curled clouds. To thy strong bidding task[108]
Ariel and all his quality.[109]

---

102  *thy schoolmaster . . . careful* Prospero is extolling the virtues of his home-schooling, yet
      clearly Miranda knows nothing of Ariel, for he puts her to sleep rather than speak to Ariel in
      front of her. Why is Prospero so keen to keep his knowledge of magic to himself, while being
      so self-congratulatory about his education of Miranda?

103  *Now my dear lady* Fortune was once my enemy and is not now.

104  *zenith* Height. The term is drawn from astrological discourse, which Prospero indicates
      throughout the speech has led him to choose the present moment to strike against his
      enemies. Zenith has the sense of the highest point reached by a celestial or other object or of
      the point in the sky or celestial sphere directly above an observer.

105  *dullness* Sleepiness.

106  *give it way* Succumb to sleep.

107  *Come away* Come here.

108  *task* Either "Give a task for Ariel and his quality" or "Ariel and all his quality work to thy
      strong bidding."

109  *quality* Other spirits.

**Prospero**                              Hast thou, spirit,
Performed to point[110] the tempest that I bade thee?                    195
**Ariel**  To every article.
I boarded the king's ship: now on the beak,[111]
Now in the waist,[112] the deck, in every cabin
I flamed amazement.[113] Sometime I'd divide,
And burn in many places—on the topmast,                              200
The yards and bowsprit[114] would I flame distinctly,
Then meet and join. Jove's lightning,[115] the precursors
O' th' dreadful thunder-claps, more momentary
And sight-outrunning[116] were not; the fire and cracks
Of sulphurous roaring the most mighty Neptune[117]                    205
Seem to besiege and make his bold waves tremble,
Yea, his dread trident shake.
**Prospero**                              My brave spirit!
Who was so firm, so constant, that this coil[118]
Would not infect his reason?
**Ariel**                              Not a soul
But felt a fever of the mad[119] and played                          210
Some tricks of desperation. All but mariners
Plunged in the foaming brine and quit the vessel,
Then all afire[120] with me: the king's son, Ferdinand,
With hair up-staring—then like reeds, not hair—
Was the first man that leapt; cried, "Hell is empty                  215
And all the devils are here."

---

110  *to point*  Precisely.
111  *beak*  Bow.
112  *waist*  Middle of the ship.
113  *flamed amazement*  Ariel caused wonder. One of the sources for *The Tempest* described the electrical phenomenon of St. Elmo's fire, which looks like flame sparking across the rigging of a sailing ship.
114  *bowsprit*  "A large spar or boom running out from the stem of the vessel, to which . . . the foremast stays are fastened." (*OED*, 3rd ed., s.v. "bowsprit," n1).
115  *Jove's lightning*  Jove, or Jupiter, was both the King of the Gods and the God of Lightning in Roman mythology.
116  *sight-outrunning*  Moving faster than can be seen.
117  *Neptune*  God of the Sea in Roman mythology.
118  *coil*  Confusion; also, a coil could be a grouping of things (here fantastical events; also, form, as in the form taken by Ariel).
119  *of the mad*  Of the kind suffered by the mad.
120  *afire*  Throughout the play, Ariel is associated with different elements, not just air. This ambiguity of elemental form feeds into the ambiguity regarding Ariel's gender, intentions, and feelings towards Prospero.

**Prospero**                                      Why that's my spirit!
But was not this nigh shore?[121]
**Ariel**                                      Close by, my master.
**Prospero**  But are they, Ariel, safe?
**Ariel**                                      Not a hair perished.
On their sustaining garments[122] not a blemish,
But fresher than before; and, as thou bad'st me,                    220
In troops[123] I have dispersed them 'bout the isle.
The king's son have I landed by himself,
Whom I left cooling of the air with sighs
In an odd[124] angle of the isle, and sitting,
His arms in this sad knot.
**Prospero**                                      Of the king's ship                    225
The mariners say how thou hast disposed,
And all the rest o' th' fleet.
**Ariel**                                      Safely in harbour
Is the king's ship; in the deep nook, where once
Thou called'st me up at midnight to fetch dew
From the still-vexed Bermoothes,[125] there she's hid,                    230
The mariners all under hatches stowed,[126]
Who, with a charm joined to their suffered labour,[127]
I have left asleep. And for the rest o' th' fleet
Which I dispersed, they all have met again
And are upon the Mediterranean float,[128]                    235
Bound sadly home for Naples,
Supposing that they saw the king's ship wrecked
And his great person perish.
**Prospero**                                      Ariel, thy charge
Exactly is performed; but there's more work.
What is the time o' th' day?
**Ariel**                                      Past the mid-season.[129]                    240

---

121  *was not . . . shore*  Wasn't this close to shore?
122  *sustaining garments*  They sustain because they protect from the elements, not because they
     serve as improvised life preservers.
123  *troops*  Small groups.
124  *odd*  Out of the way.
125  *Bermoothes*  Bermudas.
126  *stowed*  Fastened under the hatches like cargo.
127  *their suffered labour*  The mariners are asleep partially because of a charm and partially
     because of the exhaustion from their toiling through the storm.
128  *float*  Sea.
129  *mid-season*  Noon.

*Prospero*  At least two glasses.[130] The time 'twixt six and now
   Must by us both be spent most preciously.
*Ariel*  Is there more toil? Since thou dost give me pains,
   Let me remember[131] thee what thou hast promised,
   Which is not yet performed me.
*Prospero*                           How now? Moody?[132]                    245
   What is't thou canst demand?
*Ariel*                     My liberty.
*Prospero*  Before the time be out?[133] No more.
*Ariel*                               I prithee
   Remember I have done thee worthy service,
   Told thee no lies, made thee no mistakings, served
   Without or grudge or grumblings. Thou did'st promise          250
   To bate[134] me a full year.
*Prospero*                    Dost thou forget
   From what a torment I did free thee?
*Ariel*                              No.
*Prospero*  Thou dost, and think'st it much to tread the ooze
   Of the salt deep,
   To run upon the sharp wind of the north,                      255
   To do me business in the veins o' th' earth
   When it is baked with frost.
*Ariel*                        I do not, sir.
*Prospero*  Thou liest, malignant thing! Hast thou forgot
   The foul witch Sycorax,[135] who with age and envy
   Was grown into a hoop?[136] Hast thou forgot her?             260
*Ariel*  No, sir.
*Prospero*       Thou hast. Where was she born? Speak, tell me.
*Ariel*  Sir, in Argier.[137]

---

130  *two glasses*  Two hourglasses past noon, that is, two p.m.
131  *remember*  Remind.
132  *Moody*  Angry; headstrong; passionate; wilful; sullen.
133  *time be out*  Ariel's relationship with Prospero would have been recognized by Renaissance
     audiences as indentured servitude, wherein one party agrees to serve another party for a lim-
     ited amount of time, usually seven years. This echoes the discussion of vassalage and homage
     from earlier in the play.
134  *bate*  As a verb, it means "to reduce." Ariel, as a slave, feels reduced through servitude.
135  *Sycorax*  This name is unique in all of Shakespeare and though many scholars have suggested
     possible sources and meanings, none have been convincing.
136  *hoop*  Sycorax was bent forward with age.
137  *Argier*  Algiers

**Prospero**  O, was she so?[138] I must
Once in a month recount what thou hast been,
Which thou forget'st. This damned witch Sycorax,
For mischiefs manifold and sorceries terrible                              265
To enter human hearing, from Argier,
Thou know'st, was banished—for one thing she did
They would not take her life.[139] Is not this true?

**Ariel**  Aye, sir.

**Prospero**  This blue-eyed hag[140] was hither brought with child,          270
And here was left by th' sailors. Thou, my slave,[141]
As thou report'st thyself, wast then her servant,
And, for[142] thou wast a spirit too delicate
To act[143] her earthy and abhorred commands,
Refusing her grand hests,[144] she did confine thee,                        275
By help of her more potent ministers
And in her most unmitigable rage,
Into a cloven pine, within which rift
Imprisoned thou did'st painfully remain
A dozen years, within which space she died                                  280
And left thee there, where thou did'st vent thy groans
As fast as millwheels strike.[145] Then was this island—
Save for the son that she did litter[146] here,
A freckled whelp[147] hag-born—not honoured with
A human shape.

**Ariel**  Yes, Caliban, her son.                                           285

---

138  *was she so*  This section reminds us that everything Prospero knows about Sycorax is from Ariel and Caliban.

139  *take her life*  They would not take her life because she was pregnant. Early modern penal practice was to never execute a woman if she was pregnant, which meant that many women convicted of capital crimes "pled their belly" or claimed to be pregnant to stave off execution.

140  *blue-eyed hag*  Blue-eyed witch, Sycorax. This phrase has puzzled commentators who have sought to explain it in terms of race (Sycorax transcends racial characteristics) and cosmetics or age (Sycorax had blue eyelids). No single explanation has been wholly satisfactory.

141  *slave*  As noted above, the relationship between Prospero and Ariel is one of indentured servitude, which was a kind of slavery, despite the fixed term. In such a relationship, the master had exceptional powers of command over the indentured servant, bordering on the absolutism of slavery as practiced in later centuries.

142  *for*  Because.

143  *act*  Enact, carry out.

144  *hests*  Behests, commands.

145  *millwheels strike*  Ariel groaned as often as the blades of a millwheel strike the waters of a river.

146  *litter*  Give birth to, like an animal.

147  *whelp*  The offspring of a dangerous or monstrous creature. "Son of a bitch."

*Prospero* Dull thing,[148] I say so—he, that Caliban
    Whom now I keep in service. Thou best know'st
    What torment I did find thee in. Thy groans
    Did make wolves howl and penetrate the breasts
    Of ever-angry bears[149]—it was a torment          290
    To lay upon the damned, which Sycorax
    Could not again undo. It was mine art,
    When I arrived and heard thee, that made gape
    The pine and let thee out.
*Ariel*                   I thank thee, master.
*Prospero* If thou more murmur'st, I will rend an oak      295
    And peg thee in his knotty entrails till
    Thou hast howled away twelve winters.
*Ariel*                       Pardon, master.
    I will be correspondent to command
    And do my spiriting gently.[150]
*Prospero*               Do so, and after two days
    I will discharge thee.
*Ariel*              That's my noble master.      300
    What shall[151] I do? Say what? What shall I do?
*Prospero* Go make thyself like a nymph o' th' sea.[152]
    Be subject to no sight but thine and mine, invisible[153]
    To every eyeball else. Go take this shape
    And hither come in't. Go! Hence with diligence!    305

                           *Exit [ARIEL.]*

[*To MIRANDA.*] Awake, dear heart, awake! Thou hast slept well.
Awake!

---

148  *Dull thing*  It is unclear whether Prospero is continuing to insult Caliban or is directing this at Ariel.

149  *Thy groans . . . bears*  Ariel's cries aroused sympathy from even vicious animals. The bloody "sport" of bear-baiting, where a bear would be staked to the ground and dogs released to see which survived, was practiced just a few metres from theatres like Shakespeare's Globe. Thus, the groans of bears and barking of dogs would have been familiar to playgoers.

150  *gently*  Softly, with submission.

151  *shall*  Must.

152  *nymph o' th' sea*  Again, Ariel is not always associated with the element of air. Here Ariel is taking on the form of a water spirit.

153  *invisible*  In Shakespeare's day, invisibility on stage was indicated by wearing a certain cloak. In the inventory of properties from the theatre of Shakespeare's rivals, there is an entry for an "invisibility cloak."

**Miranda**     The strangeness of your story put
  Heaviness[154] in me.
**Prospero**                 Shake it off. Come on;
  We'll visit Caliban, my slave, who never
  Yields us kind answer.
**Miranda**                     'Tis a villain,[155] sir,          310
  I do not love to look on.
**Prospero**                     But, as 'tis,
  We cannot miss[156] him. He does make our fire,
  Fetch in our wood, and serves in offices
  That profit us. What ho, slave! Caliban!
  Thou earth,[157] thou, speak!
**Caliban** [*Within.*]              There's wood enough within.     315
**Prospero** Come forth I say, there's other business for thee.
  Come, thou tortoise, when?

  *Enter ARIEL like a water-nymph.*

  Fine apparition! My quaint[158] Ariel,
  Hark in thine ear. [*Whispers.*]
**Ariel**                     My lord it shall be done.

                                              *Exit [ARIEL.]*

**Prospero** Thou poisonous slave, got by the devil himself     320
  Upon thy wicked dam, come forth!

  *Enter CALIBAN.*

**Caliban** As wicked dew as e'er my mother brushed
  With raven's feather from unwholesome fen
  Drop on you both! A southwest[159] blow on ye
  And blister you all o'er!                                    325

---

154  *Heaviness*  Sleepiness.
155  *villain*  Multiple meanings are possible. "Villain" was originally used to denote any rustic, low-born servant or slave, but gathered the additional modern connotations. As is shortly explained, Caliban tried to rape Miranda.
156  *miss*  Do without.
157  *earth*  This reference is one of the reasons Ariel is often associated with the air, as earth and air were opposite elements. As Caliban is earth, Ariel, it is supposed, must be air, yet this reading ignores the multiple forms Ariel takes throughout the play.
158  *quaint*  Clever, skilful, ingenious.
159  *southwest*  Southwest winds were damp and hot, thus thought to spread disease.

**Prospero**  For this, be sure, tonight thou shalt have cramps,
    Side-stitches that shall pen thy breath up. Urchins[160]
    Shall, for that vast of night that they may work,
    All exercise on thee; thou shalt be pinched
    As thick as honeycomb,[161] each pinch more stinging    330
    Than bees that made 'em.

**Caliban**                        I must eat my dinner.
    This island's mine by Sycorax my mother,
    Which thou tak'st from me. When thou cam'st first,
    Thou strok'st me and made much of me; wouldst give me
    Water with berries in't, and teach me how    335
    To name the bigger light, and how the less,[162]
    That burn by day and night; and then I loved thee
    And showed thee all the qualities o' th' isle,
    The fresh springs, brine pits, barren place and fertile—
    Cursed be I that did so! All the charms[163]    340
    Of Sycorax, toads, beetles, bats, light on you!
    For I am all the subjects that you have,
    Which first was mine own king, and here you sty me
    In this hard rock, whiles you do keep from me
    The rest o' th' island.

**Prospero**                Thou most lying slave,    345
    Whom stripes[164] may move, not kindness! I have used thee—
    Filth as thou art—with human care, and lodged thee
    In mine own cell, till thou did'st seek to violate
    The honour of my child.

**Caliban**             O ho, O ho! Would't had been done!
    Thou did'st prevent me—I had peopled else    350
    This isle with Calibans.

---

160  *Urchins*  Spirits in the shape of hedgehogs. Many of the spirits that Caliban talks about are in the shape of hedgehogs. Indeed, Caliban's lodgings suggest the proverb, "Hedgehogs lodge among thorns because themselves are prickly." Morris Palmer Tilley, *Dictionary of the Proverbs in England in the Sixteenth and Seventeenth Centuries* (Ann Arbor, MI: University of Michigan Press, 1950), H368.

161  *thick as honeycomb*  Caliban will be pinched as closely as a bee pinches the wax to form a honeycomb.

162  *bigger light . . . less*  The sun and the moon. See Gen. 1.16: "And God made two great lyghtes: a greater lyght to rule the day, and the lesse lyght to rule the nyght" (*Bishops' Bible*, 1568).

163  *charms*  Spells.

164  *stripes*  Lashes from whipping.

**Prospero**                           Abhorred slave,
  Which any print[165] of goodness wilt[166] not take,
  Being capable of all ill! I pitied thee,
  Took pains to make thee speak, taught thee each hour
  One thing or other. When thou did'st not, savage,                    355
  Know thine own meaning, but wouldst gabble like
  A thing most brutish, I endowed thy purposes
  With words that made them known. But thy vile race[167]—
  Though thou did'st learn—had that in't which good natures
  Could not abide to be with; therefore wast thou                      360
  Deservedly confined into this rock,
  Who hadst deserved more than a prison.
**Caliban**  You taught me language; and my profit on't
  Is I know how to curse. The red plague[168] rid you
  For learning me your language!
**Prospero**                           Hag-seed,[169] hence!                365
  Fetch us in fuel, and be quick, thou'rt best,[170]
  To answer other business[171]—shrug'st thou, malice?
  If thou neglect'st or dost unwillingly
  What I command, I'll rack thee with old cramps,
  Fill all thy bones with aches,[172] make thee roar,                   370
  That beasts shall tremble at thy din.
**Caliban**                            No, pray thee.

  [*Aside.*]

  I must obey. His art is of such power,

---

165  *print*  Imprint, with the further implication of corporal punishment.
166  *wilt*  Will.
167  *race*  "Race" had not developed its modern meaning at this point. The term was used as a general classification tool. One could have a race of glasses or a race of books as much as a race of people.
168  *red plague*  A general term applied to any number of diseases that resulted in bloody pustules.
169  *hag-seed*  Caliban's mother, Sycorax, is described as a "hag," and Caliban is of her "seed." In some early modern medical theories, women, as well as men, were thought to produce "seeds," both of which were necessary for conception. This was not a popular theory, however, as it proposed women had an active part in the generation of offspring.
170  *thou'rt best*  You had better.
171  *answer other business*  To do other work.
172  *aches*  Pronounced "aitches" in seventeenth-century pronunciation.

It would control my dam's god, Setebos,[173]
And make a vassal of him.

**Prospero**                    So, slave, hence!

                                              *Exit CALIBAN.*

*Enter FERDINAND and ARIEL, invisible, playing[174] and singing.*

**Ariel**  *Song.*
  Come unto these yellow sands,                    375
   And then take hands;
  Curtsied when you have, and kissed
   The wild waves whist;[175]
  Foot it featly[176] here and there,
   And, sweet sprites, bear                    380
  The burden. Hark, hark!
*Burden[177] dispersedly[178]* [*within.*] Bow-wow
   The watch-dogs bark!
    Bow-wow
   Hark, hark! I hear                    385
  The strain of strutting Chanticleer[179]
   Cry, Cock-a-diddle-dow.
   Cry, Cock-a-diddle-dow.

**Ferdinand**  Where should this music be? I' th' air or th' earth?
It sounds no more, and sure it waits[180] upon                    390
Some god o' th' island. Sitting on a bank,
Weeping again the king my father's wreck,
This music crept by me upon the waters,
Allaying both their fury and my passion
With its sweet air.[181] Thence I have followed it—                    395

---

173  *Setebos*  A Patagonian god, first mentioned in English as "Settaboth" or "Settaboh" in the journals of Francis Fletcher, who was the chaplain on Sir Francis Drake's circumnavigation of the globe in 1577–80.
174  playing  Presumably playing a stringed instrument, though Ariel later enters playing a tabor and a pipe.
175  *whist*  Become silent.
176  *foot it featly*  Dance spritely.
177  burden  "The refrain or chorus of a song" (*OED*, 3rd ed., s.v. "burden," n10).
178  dispersedly  Sung at various places around the stage, including within the tiring house or offstage.
179  *Chanticleer*  The name of the rooster appearing in the fables of Reynard the Fox, a version of which appears in Chaucer's "Nun's Priest's Tale."
180  *waits*  Attends.
181  *air*  Tune.

Or it hath drawn me rather—but 'tis gone.
No, it begins again.

*Ariel  Song.*

 Full fathom five[182] thy father lies,
 Of his bones are coral made;
 Those are pearls that were his eyes,     400
 Nothing of him that doth fade
 But doth suffer a sea-change
 Into something rich and strange.
 Sea-nymphs hourly ring his knell.
  *Burden.*
 Ding-dong.     405

*Ferdinand*  Hark, now I hear them.

*Ariel*         Ding-dong bell.

*Ferdinand*  The ditty does remember my drowned father.
This is no mortal business, nor no sound
That the earth owes—I hear it now above me.

*Prospero*  The fringed curtains of thine eye[183] advance,  410
And say what thou seest yond.[184]

*Miranda*       What is't? A spirit?
Lord, how it looks about. Believe me, sir,
It carries a brave[185] form. But 'tis a spirit.

*Prospero*  No, wench, it eats and sleeps and hath such senses
As we have—such.[186] This gallant which thou seest  415
Was in the wreck, and, but he's something stained
With grief—that's beauty's canker—thou might'st call him
A goodly[187] person. He hath lost his fellows
And strays about to find 'em.

*Miranda*      I might call him
A thing divine, for nothing natural     420
I ever saw so noble.

---

182 *Full fathom five*  About nine metres or thirty feet. A fathom is two yards or 1.8288 metres. The lyrics were set to music by the early modern court musician Robert Johnson, son of John Johnson, lutenist to Queen Elizabeth I.

183 *fringed curtains . . . eye*  Eyelashes.

184 *yond*  Yonder, over there.

185 *brave*  Handsome.

186 *we have—such*  The dash represents a pause in speech that is indicated in the Folio with a colon. Prospero reassures Miranda that Ferdinand is, actually, not a spirit.

187 *goodly*  Handsome.

*Prospero* [*Aside.*]
                 It goes on, I see,
As my soul prompts it. Spirit, fine spirit! I'll free thee
Within two days for this.
*Ferdinand*              Most sure, the goddess
On whom these airs attend. Vouchsafe[188] my prayer
May know if you remain upon this island,               425
And that you will some good instruction give
How I may bear me here. My prime request,
Which I do last pronounce, is—O you wonder!—
If you be maid[189] or no?
*Miranda*             No wonder, sir,
But certainly a maid.
*Ferdinand*          My language! Heavens!        430
I am the best[190] of them that speak this speech,
Were I but where 'tis spoken.[191]
*Prospero*             How? The best?
What wert thou, if the King of Naples heard thee?
*Ferdinand* A single[192] thing, as I am now, that wonders
To hear thee speak of Naples. He does hear me,     . 435
And that he does, I weep. Myself am Naples,
Who with mine eyes, never since at ebb,[193] beheld
The king my father wrecked.
*Miranda*             Alack, for mercy!
*Ferdinand* Yes, faith, and all his lords, the Duke of Milan
And his brave son[194] being twain.
*Prospero* [*Aside.*]
                  The Duke of Milan      440
And his more braver daughter could control thee,
If now 'twere fit to do't. At the first sight
They have changed eyes.[195] Delicate Ariel,

---

188  *Vouchsafe*  Grant.
189  *maid*  An unmarried woman (and thus a virgin), though Ferdinand is also asking if she is human.
190  *best*  First in rank.
191  *Were I . . . spoken*  Italy.
192  *single*  Solitary. With the apparent death of his father, Ferdinand believes that he is the King of Naples.
193  *ebb*  Low tide.
194  *Yes, faith . . . twain*  Ferdinand says that everyone, including the Duke of Milan (Antonio) and his son, were killed. Nowhere else in the play is Antonio's son mentioned.
195  *changed eyes*  Exchanged loving looks.

I'll set thee free for this. [*To FERDINAND.*] A word, good sir:
I fear you have done yourself some wrong. A word.                                445

*Miranda*  Why speaks my father so ungently? This
    Is the third man that e'er I saw, the first
    That e'er I sighed for. Pity move my father
    To be inclined my way!

*Ferdinand*              O, if a virgin,[196]
    And your affection not gone forth, I'll make you                       450
    The Queen of Naples.

*Prospero*            Soft,[197] sir, one word more.
    [*Aside.*] They are both in either's powers, but this swift business
    I must uneasy[198] make, lest too light winning
    Make the prize light.[199]—One word more: I charge thee
    That thou attend me. Thou dost here usurp                               455
    The name thou ow'st not, and hast put thyself
    Upon this island as a spy, to win it
    From me, the lord on't.[200]

*Ferdinand*              No, as I am a man!

*Miranda*  There's nothing ill can dwell in such a temple.
    If the ill spirit have so fair a house,
    Good things will strive to dwell with't.[201]                           460

*Prospero*                Follow me.
    Speak not you for him; he's a traitor. Come,
    I'll manacle thy neck and feet together.
    Sea-water shalt thou drink; thy food shall be
    The fresh-brook mussels,[202] withered roots and husks                  465
    Wherein the acorn cradled. Follow.

*Ferdinand*              No,
    I will resist such entertainment[203] till
    Mine enemy has more power.

*He draws, and is charmed from moving.*

---

196  *if a virgin*  Ferdinand has already asked her this question and received an answer. He shows a remarkable lack of tact, yet a woman's virginity was what made her a marriageable commodity in aristocratic circles.

197  *Soft*  A command meaning "be silent."

198  *uneasy*  Difficult.

199  *light . . . light*  Easily won, the prize would not be regarded well.

200  *on't*  Of it.

201  *There's nothing . . . with't*  Compare this description with that of Caliban.

202  *fresh-brook mussels*  These are inedible.

203  *entertainment*  Treatment.

**Miranda**                    O dear father,
Make not too rash[204] a trial of him, for
He's gentle and not fearful.[205]
**Prospero**                    What? I say,                                    470
My foot[206] my tutor? Put thy sword up, traitor;
Who mak'st a show but dar'st not strike, thy conscience
Is so possessed with guilt. Come from thy ward,[207]
For I can here disarm thee with this stick
And make thy weapon drop.
**Miranda**                    Beseech you, father—                           475
**Prospero**  Hence! Hang not on my garments.
**Miranda**                              Sir, have pity;
I'll be his surety.[208]
**Prospero**          Silence! One word more
Shall make me chide thee, if not hate thee. What,
An advocate for an imposter? Hush!
Thou think'st there is no more such shapes as he,               480
Having seen but him and Caliban. Foolish wench!
To th' most of men this is a Caliban
And they to him are angels.
**Miranda**                    My affections
Are then most humble. I have no ambition
To see a goodlier man.[209]
**Prospero**  [*To FERDINAND.*]
                              Come on, obey.                                  485
Thy nerves[210] are in their infancy again
And have no vigour in them.
**Ferdinand**              So they are.
My spirits, as in a dream, are all bound up.
My father's loss, the weakness which I feel,
The wreck of all my friends, nor this man's threats—            490
To whom I am subdued—are but light[211] to me,
Might I but through my prison once a day

---

204  *rash*  Hasty, impetuous.
205  *fearful*  Causing fear. Alternatively, cowardly.
206  *My foot*  My subordinate.
207  *ward*  Defensive posture.
208  *I'll be his surety*  I'll vouch for him.
209  *I have . . . man*  Compare this with Ferdinand's insistence on knowing if Miranda is a virgin.
210  *nerves*  Sinews, tendons.
211  *light*  Minor burdens.

Behold this maid. All corners else o' th' earth
Let liberty make use of space enough
Have I in such a prison.                                                    495
**Prospero** [*Aside.*] It works. [*To FERDINAND.*] Come on—
[*To ARIEL.*] Thou hast done well, fine Ariel! Follow me;
Hark what thou else shalt do me.[212]
**Miranda** [*To FERDINAND.*]
                                        Be of comfort.
My father's of a better nature, sir,
Than he appears by speech. This is unwonted[213]                           500
Which now came from him.
**Prospero**                              Thou shalt be free
As mountain winds; but then exactly do
All points of my command.
**Ariel**                              To th' syllable.
**Prospero** Come, follow. [*To MIRANDA.*] Speak not for him.

                                                    [*Exeunt.*]

# ACT TWO, SCENE ONE (2.1)

We see the members of the court of ALONSO, whom we were first introduced
to in 1.1, wandering aimlessly about the island. GONZALO tries to cheer up
his monarch, while SEBASTIAN and ANTONIO make snide remarks to one
another about the aged counsellor. During the conversation, we learn that the
court was returning from the city of Algiers, where the king had just married his
daughter to an African, a decision that SEBASTIAN loathes. ALONSO cannot
be brought out of his depression at having apparently lost his son, FERDINAND,
to the sea, even when GONZALO tells a fantastic story about how he would
govern the island as a utopian commonwealth, if he had the right to control it.

Then ARIEL enters, playing music, and puts all of the court to sleep under a spell
with the exception of SEBASTIAN and ANTONIO. ANTONIO, seeing his opportunity, tries to convince SEBASTIAN to kill his brother, ALONSO, and there-
by become King of Naples. After a long conversation, where ANTONIO shows
himself to still be as dastardly a character as PROSPERO described him in the
first act, they eventually draw their swords, ready to kill the king and courtiers.

---

212 *do me* Do for me.
213 *unwonted* Unusual, unaccustomed.

When SEBASTIAN and ANTONIO are on the point of killing the king and courtiers, ARIEL breaks the spell and the others wake up. Seeing SEBASTIAN and ANTONIO with their swords drawn, they ask what happened while they were asleep. The treacherous pair claims that they heard monsters and the court continues on its way, wandering the island.

## Act Two
## Scene One

*Enter ALONSO, SEBASTIAN, ANTONIO, GONZALO, ADRIAN, FRANCISCO.*

**Gonzalo**  Beseech you, sir, be merry. You have cause—
So have we all—of joy, for our escape
Is much beyond[214] our loss. Our hint[215] of woe
Is common: every day some sailor's wife,
The masters of some merchant,[216] and the merchant          5
Have just our theme of woe; but for the miracle—
I mean our preservation—few in millions
Can speak like us. Then wisely, good sir, weigh
Our sorrow with our comfort.[217]
**Alonso**                                        Prithee, peace.[218]
**Sebastian**  [*Aside to ANTONIO.*]
He receives comfort like cold porridge.[219]                  10
**Antonio**  The visitor[220] will not give him o'er so.
**Sebastian**  Look, he's winding up the watch of his wit.
By and by it will strike.
**Gonzalo**  Sir—

---

214  *beyond*  More important than.
215  *hint*  Occasion.
216  *merchant*  Merchant vessel.
217  *weigh / Our . . . comfort*  Consider both our survival as well as our shipwreck.
218  *Prithee, peace*  Please be quiet.
219  *He receives . . . porridge*  Much of the rest of the scene until Alonso and the others fall asleep is an example of stichomythia. Stichomythia is the name of the rhetorical trope where dialogue is composed of a single line spoken by one character followed by a single line spoken by another character. It has the effect of speeding up the tempo of delivery and changes the dramatic rhythm in notable ways: one, by challenging players to deliver their lines intelligibly but at an increased pace; and two, by asking that the audience keep up with the display of wit usually in evidence in stichomythic exchanges.
220  *visitor*  In this case, Antonio is making a reference to a minor church functionary whose purpose was to visit and comfort the sick.

**Sebastian**      One. Tell.[221]

**Gonzalo**                          —when every grief is entertained      15
That's offered, comes to th' entertainer—

**Sebastian**  A dollar.[222]

**Gonzalo**  Dolour[223] comes to him, indeed. You have spoken truer than you
purposed.

**Sebastian**  You have taken it wiselier than I meant you should.      20

**Gonzalo**  Therefore, my lord—

**Antonio**  Fie, what a spendthrift is he of his tongue!

**Alonso**  [*To GONZALO.*] I prithee, spare.[224]

**Gonzalo**  Well, I have done. But yet—

**Sebastian**  He will be talking.      25

**Antonio**  Which, of he or Adrian, for a good wager, first begins to crow?[225]

**Sebastian**  The old cock.

**Antonio**  The cockerel.[226]

**Sebastian**  Done. The wager?

**Antonio**  A laughter.[227]      30

**Sebastian**  A match!

**Adrian**  Though this island seem to be desert[228]—

**Antonio**  Ha, ha, ha!

**Sebastian**  So, you're paid.

**Adrian**  Uninhabitable and almost inaccessible—      35

**Sebastian**  Yet—

**Adrian**  Yet—

**Antonio**  He could not miss't.

**Adrian**  It must needs be of subtle, tender, and delicate temperance.

**Antonio**  Temperance was a delicate wench.[229]      40

---

221  *One. Tell*  The watch of his [Gonzalo's] wit has struck one. Keep time.

222  *A dollar*  Comes in payment to the entertainer. The English name for the German silver coin,
the thaler.

223  *Dolour*  Sadness, grief. Gonzalo recognizes Sebastian's wordplay on "dollar" and turns it back
on him.

224  *spare*  End, desist, stop.

225  *Which of . . . crow?*  Based on a proverb, "the young cock crows as he the old hears" (Tilley,
*Dictionary of Proverbs*, C491).

226  *cockerel*  A young rooster.

227  *A laughter*  Proverbial: "He who laughs, wins" (Ibid., L93).

228  *desert*  In the early modern period, "desert" indicated any area where no one was living, of
whatever climate.

229  *Temperance was . . . wench*  Antonio intentionally misunderstands Adrian and misconstrues
"temperance" to be the name of a woman.

*Sebastian*  Aye, and a subtle, as he most learnedly delivered.[230]

*Adrian*  The air breathes upon us here most sweetly.

*Sebastian*  As if it had lungs, and rotten ones.

*Antonio*  Or as 'twere perfumed by a fen.[231]

*Gonzalo*  Here is everything advantageous to life.                    45

*Antonio*  True, save means to live.

*Sebastian*  Of that there's none or little.

*Gonzalo*  How lush and lusty the grass looks! How green!

*Antonio*  The ground indeed is tawny.[232]

*Sebastian*  With an eye[233] of green in't.                           50

*Antonio*  He misses not much.[234]

*Sebastian*  No, he doth but mistake the truth totally.

*Gonzalo*  But the rarity of it is, which is indeed almost beyond credit—

*Sebastian*  As many vouched rarities[235] are.

*Gonzalo*  That our garments, being, as they were, drenched in the sea, hold        55
notwithstanding their freshness and glosses, being rather new-dyed than
stained with salt water.

*Antonio*  If but one of his pockets could speak, would it not say he lies?

*Sebastian*  Aye, or very falsely pocket up[236] his report.[237]

*Gonzalo*  Methinks our garments are now as fresh as when we put them on first   60
in Africa, at the marriage of the king's fair daughter Claribel to the King of
Tunis.

*Sebastian*  'Twas a sweet marriage, and we prosper well in our return.

*Adrian*  Tunis was never graced before with such a paragon to their queen.

*Gonzalo*  Not since widow Dido's time.[238]                          65

*Antonio*  Widow? A pox o' that! How came that widow in? Widow Dido!

*Sebastian*  What if he had said "widower Aeneas" too? Good Lord, how you
take it!

---

230  *learnedly delivered*  "Spoken with authority." Sebastian is being sarcastic.

231  *fen*  A marsh or swamp; a low and marshy or frequently flooded area of land.

232  *tawny*  Brown.

233  *eye*  Hint.

234  *He misses . . . much*  Antonio intentionally misconstrues the dialogue yet again. In this case,
he is suggesting that Gonzalo has an "eye of green," which implies jealousy or meanness of
character.

235  *rarity . . . rarities*  Exceptional or noteworthy thing.

236  *pocket up*  Conceal.

237  *his report*  Gonzalo's reputation.

238  *Dido's time*  In the ancient Roman epic *The Aeneid*, Dido, Queen of Carthage, had been married to Sychaeus and Aeneas had been married to Creusa before Dido and Aeneas met and
fell in love. In Greek and Roman sources Dido is the founder and first Queen of Carthage (now
Tunisia). When Aeneas departs Carthage on the orders of Jupiter and Mercury, she commits
suicide.

**Adrian** "Widow Dido," said you? you make me study of[239] that. She was of
    Carthage, not of Tunis.           70

**Gonzalo** This Tunis, sir, was Carthage.[240]

**Adrian** Carthage?

**Gonzalo** I assure you, Carthage.

**Antonio** His word is more than the miraculous harp.

**Sebastian** He hath raised the wall and houses too.[241]       75

**Antonio** What impossible matter will he make easy next?

**Sebastian** I think he will carry this island home in his pocket and give it his
    son for an apple.

**Antonio** And, sowing the kernels[242] of it in the sea, bring forth more islands.

**Gonzalo** I—       80

**Antonio** Why, in good time.[243]

**Gonzalo** [*To* ALONZO.] Sir, we were talking that our garments seem now as
    fresh as when we were at Tunis at the marriage of your daughter, who is
    now queen.

**Antonio** And the rarest that e'er came there.       85

**Sebastian** Bate, I beseech you, widow Dido.[244]

**Antonio** O, widow Dido! Aye, widow Dido.

**Gonzalo** Is not, sir, my doublet as fresh as the first day I wore it? I mean, in a
    sort.[245]

**Antonio** That "sort" was well fished for.[246]       90

**Gonzalo** When I wore it at your daughter's marriage—

**Alonso** You cram these words into mine ears against
    The stomach of my sense. Would I had never
    Married my daughter there, for, coming thence,

---

239  *study of*  Think about.

240  *Tunis . . . was Carthage*  While not literally true, substantially true insofar as, following the
    destruction of Carthage at the end of the Third Punic War (149–46 BCE), a neighbouring city,
    Tunis, replaced it as the primary economic and political power of the region.

241  *His word . . . too*  Antonio and Sebastian are making an oblique reference to the myth of
    Amphion, a founder of Thebes, who built the walls of Thebes by using a magical lyre or harp.
    Gonzalo, they are saying, has done Amphion one better by raising the walls and the houses
    too.

242  *kernels*  Seeds.

243  *in good time*  Draws on the homonym of "I" and "aye" in the previous line. Spoken sarcasti-
    cally, "It's about time [you agreed]!"

244  *Bate . . . Dido*  Do not mention the widow Dido again.

245  *in a sort*  To some extent.

246  *well fished for*  Long in coming. Antonio is saying that it took Gonzalo a long time to realize
    that he wasn't telling the whole truth.

My son is lost, and—in my rate[247]—she too,                                    95
Who is so far from Italy removed
I ne'er again shall see her. O thou mine heir
Of Naples and of Milan,[248] what strange fish
Hath made his meal on thee?
**Francisco**                            Sir, he may live.
I saw him beat the surges under him,                                            100
And ride upon their backs. He trod the water,
Whose enmity[249] he flung aside, and breasted
The surge most swoll'n that met him. His bold head
'Bove the contentious waves he kept and oared
Himself with his good arms in lusty stroke                                      105
To th' shore, that o'er his[250] wave-worn basis bowed,[251]
As stooping to relieve him. I not doubt
He came alive to land.
**Alonso**                            No, no, he's gone.
**Sebastian** Sir, you may thank yourself for this great loss,
That would not bless our Europe with your daughter                             110
But rather lose[252] her to an African,
Where she, at least, is banished from your eye,
Who hath cause to wet the grief on't.
**Alonso**                                Prithee, peace.
**Sebastian** You were kneeled to and importuned otherwise
By all of us, and the fair soul herself                                        115
Weighed between loathness and obedience at
Which end o' th' beam should bow. We have lost your son,
I fear, forever. Milan and Naples have
More widows in them of this business' making
Than we bring[253] men to comfort them.                                        120
The fault's your own.

---

247  *rate*  Estimation.
248  *Naples . . . Milan*  Ferdinand was to have inherited the united crowns of both Naples and
     Milan, giving impetus to Antonio and Sebastian's conspiracy.
249  *enmity*  Hostility.
250  *his*  Its (the sea's).
251  *basis bowed*  The cliffs bending down to the shore.
252  *lose*  "Lose" had both its modern meaning as well as the connotation of setting forth or
     abandoning. "You would not give your daughter to a European marriage, but lost her to an
     African union."
253  *bring*  Either Sebastian is being hopeful about their eventual rescue ("than we will bring"),
     or he is morosely referring to the number of men that have apparently been saved from the
     wreck ("than we can bring").

**Alonso**                    So is the dear'st o' th' loss.

**Gonzalo**  My lord Sebastian,
   The truth you speak doth lack some gentleness
   And time[254] to speak it in—you rub the sore
   When you should bring the plaster.[255]

**Sebastian**                    Very well.                    125

**Antonio**  And most chirurgeonly![256]

**Gonzalo**  It is foul weather in us all, good sir,
   When you are cloudy.

**Sebastian**              Foul weather?

**Antonio**                    Very foul.

**Gonzalo**  Had I plantation[257] of this isle, my lord—

**Antonio**  He'd sow't[258] with nettle-seed.

**Sebastian**                    Or docks, or mallows.[259]          130

**Gonzalo**  —And were the king on't, what would I do?

**Sebastian**  'Scape being drunk for want of wine.

**Gonzalo**  I' th' commonwealth[260] I would, by contraries,[261]
   Execute all things, for no kind of traffic[262]
   Would I admit; No name of magistrate;                    135
   Letters[263] should not be known; riches, poverty,
   And use of service,[264] none; contract, succession,[265]
   Bourn,[266] bound of land, tilth,[266] vineyard, none;

---

254  *time*  Appropriate time.
255  *plaster*  A kind of medical salve.
256  *chirurgeonly*  A "chirurgeon" was an alternate spelling for a surgeon, therefore "surgeonly."
257  *plantation*  A term begun to be used in Tudor times as part of the attempt to subdue Ireland. Irish plantations were owned by the English and worked by Irish peasants.
258  *sow't*  Sow the ground.
259  *nettle-seed . . . docks . . . mallows*  All were weeds, but parts of which could be used for medical purposes. John Gerard's *The Herbal or Generall Historie of Plantes* (London: Adam Islip Ioice Norton and Richard Whitakers, 1633), a seventeenth-century pharmacological treatise, describes mallows as a purgative and coagulant (932), nettles as an anti-inflammatory (704), and docks as an analgesic (388).
260  *commonwealth*  A new Tudor concept, a nation or state defined by governance for the common good of all.
261  *By contraries*  In a manner opposed to normal governance.
262  *traffic*  Commerce.
263  *Letters*  Learning and literacy.
264  *use of service*  Keeping servants.
265  *succession*  Inheritance.
266  *bourn*  A boundary. Gonzalo is referencing the controversial practice of enclosure, whereby landlords would enclose land held in common by the community for their own personal use. This practice seriously threatened traditional rural economies throughout the early modern period.
267  *tilth*  Raising crops.

No use of metal, corn, or wine, or oil;
No occupation, all men idle, all,                                                    140
And women too, but innocent and pure;[268]
No sovereignty—
**Sebastian**            Yet he would be king on't.
**Antonio** The latter end of his commonwealth forgets the beginning.
**Gonzalo** All things in common[269] nature should produce
Without sweat or endeavour. Treason, felony,                                          145
Sword, pike, knife, gun, or need of any engine[270]
Would I not have, but nature should bring forth,
Of its own kind all foison,[271] all abundance
To feed my innocent people.
**Sebastian** No marrying 'mong his subjects?                                        150
**Antonio** None, man, all idle—whores and knaves.
**Gonzalo** I would with such perfection govern, sir,
T'excel the Golden Age.[272]
**Sebastian** 'Save[273] his majesty!
**Antonio**                          Long live Gonzalo!
**Gonzalo** And—do you mark me, sir?
**Alonso**                          Prithee no more.                                 155
Thou dost talk nothing to me.
**Gonzalo** I do well believe your highness, and did it to minister occasion[274] to
these gentlemen, who are of such sensible[275] and nimble lungs that they
always  use to laugh at nothing.[277]
**Antonio** 'Twas you we laughed at.                                                 160
**Gonzalo** Who, in this kind of merry fooling, am nothing to you, so you
may continue and laugh at nothing still.

---

268  *No occupation . . . pure*  Contrary to humanist ideologies regarding idleness (modern unem-
ployment), which was thought to stem from lust and laziness.
269  *In common*  In communal use.
270  *engine*  Any mechanical device used in warfare.
271  *foison*  Plenty.
272  *the Golden Age*  The first age of man described by the Roman poet Ovid (43 BE–18 AD); an
age of heroes, when gods walked the earth.
273  *'Save*  Shortened form of "God Save." At this point in Shakespeare's career, King James VI/I
had issued a proclamation forbidding swearing and the use of the word "God" on stage.
274  *minister occasion*  Give an opportunity for laughter.
275  *sensible*  Sensitive.
276  use  Are accustomed.
277  *I do . . . at*  Gonzalo switches to prose here, indicating a change in his mental state. Is he
exhausted by the verbal sparring with Antonio and Sebastian?

**Antonio** What a blow was there given!
**Sebastian** An[278] it had not fallen flat-long.[279]
**Gonzalo** You are gentlemen of brave mettle.[280] You would lift the moon out of          165
her sphere, if she would continue in it five weeks without changing.[281]

*Enter ARIEL, [invisible,] playing solemn music.*

**Sebastian** We would so, and then go a bat-fowling.[282]
**Antonio** Nay, good my lord, be not angry.
**Gonzalo** No, I warrant you, I will not adventure my discretion so weakly.[283]
Will you laugh me asleep, for I am very heavy.[284]          170
**Antonio** Go sleep, and hear us.

*All sleep except ALONSO, SEBASTIAN, and ANTONIO.*

**Alonso** What, all so soon asleep? I wish mine eyes
Would, with themselves, shut up my thoughts. I find
They are inclined to do so.
**Sebastian**                    Please you, sir,
Do not omit[285] the heavy offer of it.[286]          175
It seldom visits sorrow; when it doth,
It is a comforter.
**Antonio**                    We two, my lord,
Will guard your person while you take your rest,
And watch your safety.
**Alonso**                    Thank you. Wondrous heavy.[287]

*[ALONSO sleeps. Exit ARIEL.]*

---

278 *An* If.
279 *flat-long* To fall on the flat of a sword.
280 *mettle* A pun on metal, carrying on Sebastian's sword imagery; someone who can handle
demanding situations as in "true mettle," someone's ability to cope with a difficult situation.
281 *You would . . . changing* It would take an extraordinary event for you to actually do anything.
282 *a bat-fowling* Poaching birds at night, by beating bushes and trees where they are sleeping
and throwing nets over them; hence, cheating or swindling. The A-prefixing verb form ("a
X-ing") was non-standard in Shakespeare's day, but still recognizable as a regional variation.
Today, it still is used in some parts of rural Appalachia and the Maritime provinces, though is
largely considered archaic (consider its use in "The Twelve Days of Christmas").
283 *Adventure my . . . weakly* Put my good judgment at risk for such light behaviour.
284 *heavy* Sleepy.
285 *omit* Disregard.
286 *it* Sleep.
287 *Wondrous heavy* [I am] very tired. The word "wondrous," however, does include the connotation of magical or supernatural causes.

*Sebastian* What a strange drowsiness possesses them!                    180
*Antonio* It is the quality o' th' climate.
*Sebastian*                              Why
    Doth it not then our eyelids sink? I find not
    Myself disposed to sleep.
*Antonio*                          Nor I. My spirits are nimble.
    They fell together all, as[288] by consent;[289]
    They dropped, as by a thunder-stroke. What might,        185
    Worthy Sebastian. O what might—? No more.
    And yet, methinks I see it in thy face,
    What thou shouldst be. Th' occasion speaks thee,[290] and
    My strong imagination sees a crown
    Dropping upon thy head.
*Sebastian*                          What, art thou waking?             190
*Antonio* Do you not hear me speak?
*Sebastian*                              I do, and surely
    It is a sleepy language and thou speak'st
    Out of thy sleep. What is it thou did'st say?
    This is a strange repose, to be asleep
    With eyes wide open—standing, speaking, moving,        195
    And yet so fast asleep.
*Antonio*                          Noble Sebastian,
    Thou let'st thy fortune sleep—die, rather; wink'st
    Whiles thou art waking.
*Sebastian*                          Thou dost snore distinctly.
    There's meaning in thy snores.
*Antonio* I am more serious than my custom. You                         200
    Must be so too, if heed me, which to do
    Trebles thee o'er.[291]
*Sebastian*                          Well? I am standing water.[292]
*Antonio* I'll teach you how to flow.
*Sebastian*                          Do so—to ebb
    Hereditary sloth instructs me.[293]

---

288  *as*  As if.
289  *consent*  Common agreement.
290  *speaks thee*  Speaks to you.
291  *Trebles thee o'er*  Triples your fortune.
292  *standing water*  Not yet moved.
293  *Hereditary sloth . . . me*  As the younger brother, I am less likely to act.

**Antonio**                                 O!
    If you but knew how you the purpose cherish                                    205
    Whiles thus you mock it,[294] how, in stripping it,
    You more invest it.[295] Ebbing men, indeed,
    Most often do so near the bottom run
    By their own fear or sloth.[296]

**Sebastian**                                 Prithee, say on.
    The setting of thine eye and cheek proclaim                                    210
    A matter from thee, and a birth, indeed,
    Which throes thee much to yield.[297]

**Antonio**                                 Thus, sir:
    Although this lord of weak remembrance, this,
    Who shall be of as little memory
    When he is earthed,[298] hath here almost persuaded—                                    215
    For he's a spirit of persuasion,[299] only
    Professes to persuade[300]—the king his son's alive,
    'Tis as impossible that he's undrowned
    And he that sleeps here swims.

**Sebastian**                                 I have no hope
    That he's undrowned.

**Antonio**                                 O, out of that "no hope"                                    220
    What great hope have you! No hope that way is
    Another way so high a hope that even
    Ambition cannot pierce a wink beyond,
    But doubt discovery there.[301] Will you grant with me
    That Ferdinand is drowned?

**Sebastian**                                 He's gone.

**Antonio**                                 Then, tell me,                                    225
    Who's the next heir of Naples?

---

294 *If you . . . it*  If you only understood how your mockery reveals the depth of your true desires.

295 *How, in . . . it*  In mocking the thing you want, you end up desiring it more.

296 *Ebbing men . . . sloth*  "Those whose fortunes are on the wane are often almost at the end of their means because they are afraid, or because they are too indolent to do anything to improve their condition" (Stevenson, *The Tempest*, 95).

297 *throes thee . . . yield*  Gives you much pain to give up.

298 *earthed*  Buried.

299 *spirit of persuasion*  Gonzalo is an expert at the rhetorical arts. Rhetoric is the art of persuasion.

300 *Professes to persuade*  Being a minister is his only occupation. The two descriptions of Gonzalo are spoken contemptuously.

301 *Ambition cannot . . . there*  The sense is that there is no higher ambition but the crown. The complicated syntax indicates Antonio's excited emotional state.

*Sebastian*                                    Claribel.
*Antonio*  She that is Queen of Tunis; she that dwells
          Ten leagues[302] beyond man's life;[303] she that from Naples
          Can have no note,[304] unless the sun were post—
          The man i' th' moon's too slow—till new-born chins          230
          Be rough and razorable—she that from[305] whom
          We all were sea-swallowed, though some cast[306] again,
          And by that destiny to perform an act
          Whereof what's past is prologue, what to come
          In yours and my discharge.[307]                             235
*Sebastian*  What stuff is this? How say you?
          'Tis true, my brother's daughter's Queen of Tunis,
          So is she heir of Naples, 'twixt which regions
          There is some space.
*Antonio*                    A space whose every cubit[308]
          Seems to cry out, "How shall that Claribel                  240
          Measure[309] us back to Naples? Keep in Tunis,
          And let Sebastian wake." Say, this were death[310]
          That now hath seized them; why, they were no worse
          Than now they are. There be that can rule Naples
          As well as he that sleeps, lords that can prate             245
          As amply and unnecessarily
          As this Gonzalo; I myself could make
          A chough[311] of as deep chat.[312] O, that you bore
          The mind that I do! What a sleep were this
          For your advancement! Do you understand me?                 250
*Sebastian*  Methinks I do.
*Antonio*                    And how does your content
          Tender your own good fortune?

---

302  *leagues*  A league is three miles or almost five kilometres.
303  *beyond man's life*  Beyond what a man can travel in a lifetime.
304  *note*  Information.
305  *from*  Coming from.
306  *cast*  Washed ashore; also, a metatheatrical reference to actors who are "cast again" or play
     two parts in the same play.
307  *discharge*  Performance, execution of a function.
308  *cubit*  An ancient unit of measurement, from the elbow to the middle fingertip.
309  *Measure*  Travel, traverse.
310  *death*  Sleep was seen as a kind of image of death. Also, in Shakespeare's day, "death" and
     "debt" were homonyms, which sets up the financial discourse that follows.
311  *chough*  A kind of jackdaw; a small bird related to the crow.
312  *chat*  Conversation.

**Sebastian**                               I remember
   You did supplant your brother Prospero.
**Antonio**                               True:
   And look how well my garments sit upon me,
   Much feater[313] than before. My brother's servants      255
   Were then my fellows; now they are my men.
**Sebastian**  But for your conscience?
**Antonio**  Aye, sir, where lies that? If 'twere a kibe,[314]
   'Twould put me to my slipper, but I feel not
   This deity in my bosom.[315] Twenty consciences,      260
   That stand 'twixt me and Milan, candied be they
   And melt ere they molest! Here lies your brother,
   No better than the earth he lies upon,
   If he were that which now he's like—that's dead—
   Whom I with this obedient steel, three inches of it,      265
   Can lay to bed forever—whiles you, doing thus,
   To the perpetual wink for aye might put
   This ancient morsel, this Sir Prudence,[316] who
   Should not upbraid our course—for all the rest
   They'll take suggestion as a cat laps milk;      270
   They'll tell the clock to any business that
   We say befits the hour.
**Sebastian**                               Thy case, dear friend,
   Shall be my precedent. As thou got'st Milan,
   I'll come by Naples. Draw thy sword! One stroke
   Shall free thee from the tribute which thou pay'st,      275
   And I the king shall love thee.
**Antonio**                               Draw together,
   And when I rear my hand do you the like,
   To fall it on Gonzalo.
**Sebastian**                               O, but one word.

[*They talk apart.*]

*Re-enter ARIEL, [invisible,] with music and song.*

---

313  *feater*  With a better fit.
314  *kibe*  An ulcer on the foot, especially the heel; a swelling or ulcerated chilblain.
315  *If 'twere . . . bosom*  If it were as an inflammation on my feet, I'd wear slippers, but I don't feel any conscience about this act.
316  *ancient morsel . . . Prudence*  Both clauses refer to Gonzalo.

*Ariel* My master through his art foresees the danger
    That you, his friend, are in, and sends me forth—        280
    For else his project dies—to keep them living.

    *Sings in GONZALO's ear.*

       While you here do snoring lie,
       Open-eyed conspiracy
          His time doth take.
       If of life you keep a care,               285
       Shake off slumber, and beware:
          Awake, awake!
*Antonio* Then let us both be sudden.
*Gonzalo* [*Waking.*]
    Now, good angels preserve the king.

    [*They wake.*]

*Alonso* Why, how now, ho! Awake! Why are you drawn?[317]    290
    Wherefore this ghastly looking?
*Gonzalo*                What's the matter?
*Sebastian* Whiles we stood here securing your repose,
    Even now we heard a hollow burst of bellowing
    Like bulls, or rather lions. Did't not wake you?
    It struck mine ear most terribly.
*Alonso*               I heard nothing.      295
*Antonio* O, 'twas a din[318] to fright a monster's ear,
    To make an earthquake! Sure, it was the roar
    Of a whole herd of lions.
*Alonso*             Heard you this, Gonzalo?
*Gonzalo* Upon mine honour, sir, I heard a humming,
    And that a strange one too, which did awake me.    300
    I shaked you, sir, and cried. As mine eyes opened,
    I saw their weapons drawn. There was a noise,
    That's verily.[319] 'Tis best we stand upon our guard,
    Or that we quit this place. Let's draw our weapons.

---

317 *Why are you drawn*  Why do you have your swords at the ready?
318 *din*  Loud, unpleasant noise, tumult.
319 *That's verily*  That's true.

*Alonso* Lead off this ground, and let's make further search
    For my poor son.
*Gonzalo*                              Heavens keep him from these beasts!
    For he is, sure, i' th' island.
*Alonso*                                         Lead away.
*Ariel*  Prospero my lord shall know what I have done.
    So, king, go safely on to seek thy son.

*Exeunt.*

# ACT TWO, SCENE TWO (2.2)

This scene begins with the remnants of the storm moving off, but still audible. CALIBAN gathers wood and complains about his treatment by PROSPERO when the court jester TRINCULO appears. CALIBAN, thinking he is a spirit sent to punish him, lies flat on the ground under his long cloak or gabardine.

TRINCULO, a jester, comes across CALIBAN and thinks he is a native of the island struck dead by a thunderbolt. He fantasizes about taking the body back to Europe, where he could put it on display and charge money from spectators. When it looks as though the tempest is about to return, he decides to hide under the cloak with CALIBAN, not realizing he is alive.

The drunken butler STEPHANO appears, singing. His song is so unmusical that CALIBAN mistakes it for one of the spirits of the island, come to chide him for working so slowly. STEPHANO discovers what appears to be a four-legged monster hiding under a cloak. Eventually, after much scatological humour, STEPHANO uncovers the two characters hiding under the cloak. TRINCULO and STEPHANO explain how they managed to survive the apparent wreck of the ship, with STEPHANO further explaining that he has recovered a barrel of liquor from the storm, which he is now drinking.

CALIBAN, thinking that STEPHANO and TRINCULO are gods because of the liquor that STEPHANO carries, devises a plan to overthrow PROSPERO and take control of the island. CALIBAN sings for joy at the thought of no longer having to serve PROSPERO.

## Act Two
## Scene Two

*Enter CALIBAN with a burden of wood.*

**Caliban** All the infections that the sun sucks up[320]
From bogs, fens, flats, on Prosper fall, and make him
By inchmeal[321] a disease!

*A noise of thunder heard.*

His spirits hear me
And yet I needs must curse. But they'll nor[322] pinch,
Fright me with urchin-shows,[323] pitch me i' th' mire,                 5
Nor lead me, like a firebrand[324] in the dark
Out of my way, unless he bid 'em; but
For every trifle are they set upon me:
Sometime like apes that mow[325] and chatter at me
And after bite me; then like hedgehogs, which                10
Lie tumbling in my barefoot way, and mount
Their pricks at my footfall; sometime am I
All wound with adders,[326] who with cloven[327] tongues
Do hiss me into madness—

*Enter TRINCULO.*

Lo, now, lo!
Here comes a spirit[328] of his, and to torment me                15
For bringing wood in slowly. I'll fall flat;[329]
Perchance[330] he will not mind me.

**Trinculo** Here's neither bush nor shrub, to bear off any weather at all, and
another storm brewing—I hear it sing i' th' wind. Yon same black cloud,

---

320 *All the . . . up* In the Renaissance, the popular theory was that infections were caused by
highly unpleasant smells, known as "miasma." The word also figures an oppressive or unpleasant atmosphere emanating from someone or something.
321 *inchmeal* Inch by inch.
322 *nor* Neither.
323 *urchin-shows* Visions of goblins and elves.
324 *firebrand* Firebrands, or embers from fires, were carried like torches at night to light the way.
325 *mow* Grimace.
326 *adders* A species of venomous snake.
327 *cloven* Cut in two.
328 *spirit* Caliban mistakes Trinculo for one of Prospero's spirits. Though Ariel is the only spirit
who speaks to Prospero, it is clear that Prospero has a number of spirits at his command.
329 *fall flat* Caliban hides under his cloak, leading to the comedy in the following sequence.
330 *Perchance* Maybe.

yon huge one, looks like a foul bombard[331] that would shed his liquor. If it    20
should thunder as it did before, I know not where to hide my head—yon
same cloud cannot choose but fall by pailfuls. What have we here—a man
or a fish?[332]—dead or alive? A fish, he smells like a fish; a very ancient and
fish-like smell; a kind of not of the newest poor-John.[333] A strange fish!
Were I in England now, as once I was, and had but this fish painted,[334] not    25
a holiday fool[335] there but would give a piece of silver. There would this
monster make a man—any strange beast there makes a man. When they
will not give a doit[336] to relieve a lame beggar, they will lay out ten to see a
dead Indian.[337] Legged like a man[338] and his fins like arms! Warm o' my
troth![339] I do now let loose my opinion, hold it no longer: this is no fish, but    30
an islander, that hath lately suffered by a thunderbolt.

*Thunder.*

Alas, the storm is come again! My best way is to creep under his
gaberdine[340]—there is no other shelter hereabouts. Misery acquaints a man
with strange bed-fellows. I will here shroud[341] till the dregs of the storm be
past.    35

*He crawls under CALIBAN's cloak.*

*Enter STEPHANO, singing: a bottle in his hand.*

**Stephano**          I shall no more to sea, to sea,
                     Here shall I die ashore—
This is a very scurvy[342] tune to sing at a man's funeral. Well, here's my
comfort.

---

331  *bombard*  A leather jug for carrying liquor.
332  *or a fish*  One of the source texts for *The Tempest*, Strachey's *Wracke and Redemption of Sir
     Thomas Giles*, suggests a similar confusion over how to classify tortoises (Geoffrey Bullough,
     *Narrative and Dramatic Sources of Shakespeare* vol. 8 [New York: Routledge and Kegan Paul,
     1975], 285). It is possible that Caliban is here supposed to look similar to a tortoise under its
     shell.
333  *poor-John*  Dried fish.
334  *painted*  Trinculo imagines painting the fish on a sign to advertise it.
335  *holiday fool*  Someone on holiday, thus more likely to be parted from their money.
336  *doit*  Half a farthing. A farthing was a quarter of a pence.
337  *dead Indian*  As described in greater detail in the introduction, following Martin Frobisher's
     1576 expedition Aboriginal peoples of North America were brought back to England, living or
     dead, to be displayed.
338  *Legged like a man*  The fish (Caliban) has legs.
339  *o' my troth*  A minor oath; a modern equivalent might be "holy cow!"
340  *gaberdine*  A long cloak for men. In Shakespeare's England it was associated with racial
     minorities such as Jews and the Irish.
341  *shroud*  Hide, shelter.
342  *scurvy*  Worthless, contemptible; also, a disease caused by lack of vitamin C, associated with
     long sea voyages.

*Drinks.*

*Sings.*

> The master, the swabber,[342] the boatswain and I,          40
>     The gunner, and his mate,
> Loved Moll, Meg, and Marian, and Margery,
>     But none of us cared for Kate.
> For she had a tongue with a tang,[343]
> Would cry to a sailor, "Go hang!"          45
She loved not the savour of tar nor of pitch,
Yet a tailor might scratch her where'er she did itch.[344]
>     Then to sea, boys, and let her go hang!
This is a scurvy tune too, but here's my comfort.

*Drinks.*

**Caliban**  Do not torment me! O!          50

**Stephano**  What's the matter? Have we devils here? Do you put tricks upon's with savages and men of Ind?[345] Ha? I have not 'scaped drowning to be afeard now of your four legs; for it hath been said, "As proper a man as ever went on four legs cannot make him give ground."[346] And it shall be said so again, while Stephano breathes at's[347] nostrils.          55

**Caliban**  The spirit torments me! O!

**Stephano**  This is some monster of the isle with four legs, who hath got, as I take it, an ague.[348] Where the devil should he learn our language?[349] I will give him some relief, if it be but for that. If I can recover[350] him, and keep him tame and get to Naples with him, he's a present for any emperor that ever trod on neat's leather.[351]          60

**Caliban**  Do not torment me, prithee! I'll bring my wood home faster.

---

343  *swabber*  A seaman who mops the deck.
344  *tang*  Sting.
345  *She loved . . . itch*  Kate would sleep with a tailor but not with a sailor.
346  *Ind*  Whether this is supposed to refer to the West Indies (Caribbean) or the East Indies (India and modern Malaysia/Indonesia) is unclear. Either way, the local inhabitants of both areas were considered to be savages by the early modern English.
347  *As proper . . . ground*  Proverbial. "As good a Man . . . as ever went on legs" (Tilley, *Dictionary of Proverbs*, M66).
348  *at's*  At his. Stephano is referring to himself in the third person.
349  *ague*  A fever or illness.
350  *our language*  Stephano hears Caliban speaking Italian, which he has learned from Prospero.
351  *recover*  Revive.
352  *neat's leather*  Particularly supple cow hide.

***Stephano*** He's in his fit now, and does not talk after the wisest.[353] He shall taste
of my bottle. If he have never drunk wine afore, will go near to remove[354]
his fit. If I can recover him and keep him tame, I will not take too much for    65
him;[355] he shall pay for him that hath him, and that soundly.[356]

***Caliban*** Thou dost me yet but little hurt. Thou wilt anon, I know it by thy
trembling. Now Prosper works upon thee.

***Stephano*** Come on your ways. Open your mouth—here is that which will
give language to you, cat.[357] Open your mouth—this will shake your    70
shaking, I can tell you, and that soundly. [*CALIBAN drinks.*] You cannot
tell who's your friend—open your chaps[358] again.

***Trinculo*** I should know that voice. It should be—but he is drowned, and these
are devils—O, defend me!

***Stephano*** Four legs and two voices—a most delicate monster! His forward    75
voice now is to speak well of his friend, his backward voice is to utter foul
speeches and to detract.[359] If all the wine in my bottle will recover him, I
will help his ague. Come. [*CALIBAN drinks.*] Amen! I will pour some in
thy other mouth.[360]

***Trinculo*** Stephano!    80

***Stephano*** Doth thy other mouth call me? Mercy, mercy! This is a devil, and no
monster. I will leave him; I have no long spoon.[361]

***Trinculo*** Stephano! If thou be'st Stephano, touch me, and speak to me, for I am
Trinculo—be not afeard—thy good friend Trinculo.

***Stephano*** If thou be'st Trinculo, come forth. I'll pull thee bythe lesser legs—if    85
any be Trinculo's legs, these are they. [*Pulls TRINCULO from under the*

---

353  *does not . . . wisest*  Caliban's words do not make sense to Stephano, even though they are in
Italian.

354  *remove*  Take away.

355  *I will . . . him*  Stephano can charge whatever he likes for Caliban as a curiosity. This same
kind of traffic in the bodies of Aboriginals is mentioned by Montaigne and discussed in the
introduction.

356  *soundly*  Dearly.

357  *here is . . . cat*  Proverbial. "Ale that would make a cat speak" (Tilley, *Dictionary of Proverbs*,
A99). Good liquor can make anything talk.

358  *chaps*  Jaws.

359  *his backward . . . detract*  Shakespeare was fond of fart jokes. Scatological humour appears
throughout his plays, usually (though not exclusively) in the mouths of lower-class characters.

360  *thy other mouth*  There is, of course, the bawdy connotation that "other mouth" means
"anus," but this also provides internal stage directions for how the scene is to be played.
Trinculo's head is hidden under the gaberdine between Caliban's legs, which, when Stephano
moves to feed the other mouth, sets up a comic reveal.

361  *long spoon*  Proverbial. "He must have a long spoon who eats with the devil" (Ibid., S771).

*cloak.*] Thou art very Trinculo indeed! How cam'st thou to be the siege[362]
of this mooncalf?[363] Can he vent[364] Trinculos?

**Trinculo** I took him to be killed with a thunderstroke. But art thou not
drowned, Stephano? I hope now thou art not drowned. Is the storm            90
overblown? I hid me under the dead mooncalf's gaberdine for fear of the
storm. And art thou living, Stephano? O Stephano, two Neapolitans
'scaped!

**Stephano** Prithee do not turn me about; my stomach is not constant.

**Caliban** These be fine things, an if[365] they be not sprites.            95
That's a brave god, and bears celestial liquor.
I will kneel to him.

**Stephano** How did'st thou 'scape? How cam'st thou hither? Swear by this bottle
how thou cam'st hither—I escaped upon a butt of sack[366] which the sailors
heaved o'erboard—by this bottle, which I made of the bark of a tree with    100
mine own hands since I was cast ashore.

**Caliban** I'll swear upon that bottle to be thy true subject, for the liquor is not
earthly.

**Stephano** Here. Swear then how thou escaped'st.

**Trinculo** Swum ashore. man, like a duck. I can swim like a duck, I'll be sworn.  105

**Stephano** Here, kiss the book.[367] [*Gives TRINCULO the bottle.*] Though thou
canst swim like a duck, thou art made like a goose.[368]

**Trinculo** O Stephano, hast any more of this?

**Stephano** The whole butt, man. My cellar is in a rock by the seaside where my
wine is hid. How now, mooncalf, how does thine ague?                        110

**Caliban** Hast thou not dropped from heaven?

**Stephano** Out o' th' moon, I do assure thee. I was the man
i' th' moon when time was.[369]

**Caliban** I have seen thee in her, and I do adore thee.
My mistress showed me thee, and thy dog and thy bush.[370]                  115

---

362 *siege* Literally, "shit."
363 *mooncalf* Misshapen birth, monstrous prodigy, abortion, fool.
364 *vent* Fart.
365 *an if* If.
366 *butt of sack* Cask of sweet white wine.
367 *kiss the book* To kiss the Bible was a sign of loyalty in a feudal system. Here, it refers to taking another drink from the bottle.
368 *made like a goose* Geese were proverbially unsteady on their feet, thus this may be an internal stage direction for Trinculo falling down.
369 *when time was* Once upon a time.
370 *dog . . . bush* According to English folk tradition, the man in the moon was banished there
  for having gathered wood on a Sunday. He was banished with the thorn bush he gathered
  and his dog, who accompanied him.

**Stephano** Come, swear to that. Kiss the book. I will furnish[371]
  it anon with new contents. Swear!

[*CALIBAN drinks.*]

**Trinculo** By this good light, this is a very shallow[372] monster!
  I afeard of him? A very weak monster! The man i' th' moon!
  A most poor credulous monster! Well drawn,[373] monster, in good sooth![374]  120
**Caliban** I'll show thee every fertile inch o' th' island—and I will kiss thy foot.
  I prithee, be my god.
**Trinculo** By this light, a most perfidious and drunken monster! When's god's
  asleep, he'll rob his bottle.
**Caliban** I'll kiss thy foot. I'll swear myself thy subject.  125
**Stephano** Come on, then, down, and swear.
**Trinculo** I shall laugh myself to death at this puppy-headed monster.[375] A most
  scurvy monster! I could find in my heart to beat him—
**Stephano** Come, kiss.[376]
**Trinculo** —But that the poor monster's in drink. An abominable monster!  130
**Caliban** I'll show thee the best springs; I'll pluck thee berries;
  I'll fish for thee and get thee wood enough.
  A plague upon the tyrant that I serve!
  I'll bear him no more sticks, but follow thee,
  Thou wondrous man.  135
**Trinculo** A most ridiculous monster, to make a wonder of a poor drunkard!
**Caliban** I prithee, let me bring thee where crabs[377] grow,
  And I with my long nails will dig thee pig-nuts,[378]
  Show thee a jay's nest and instruct thee how
  To snare the nimble marmoset.[379] I'll bring thee  140
  To clust'ring filberts[380] and sometimes I'll get thee
  Young scamels[381] from the rock. Wilt thou go with me?

---

371 *furnish* Resupply.
372 *shallow* Credulous, believes things easily.
373 *Well drawn* Caliban has taken a very large drink from the bottle.
374 *on good sooth* Indeed, in truth.
375 *puppy-headed monster* In some productions, because of this line, Caliban has been shown
   with long, floppy ears, yet the original meaning of "puppy-headed" was "simple" or "stupid."
376 *kiss* Drink.
377 *crabs* Either crabapples or the shellfish.
378 *pig-nuts* Not "peanuts" but a type of sweet tuber that grows in Western Europe.
379 *marmoset* A small monkey.
380 *filberts* Hazelnuts.
381 *scamels* Exact meaning is uncertain, but possibly a mussel or a bird.

**Stephano**  I prithee now, lead the way without any more talking. Trinculo, the
king and all our company else being drowned, we will inherit here.
[*To CALIBAN.*] Here, bear my bottle. Fellow Trinculo, we'll fill him[382] by          145
and by again.

**Caliban**  *CALIBAN sings drunkenly.*
Farewell, master, farewell, farewell!

**Trinculo**  A howling monster; a drunken monster!

**Caliban**  No more dams[383] I'll make for fish          150
Nor fetch in firing at requiring,[384]
Nor scrape trencher,[385] nor wash dish:
  'Ban, 'Ban, Ca-Caliban
  Has a new master—get a new man.
Freedom, hey-day![386] Hey-day, freedom! Freedom, hey-day,          155
freedom!

**Stephano**  O brave[387] monster! Lead the way!

[*Exeunt.*]

# ACT THREE, SCENE ONE (3.1)

FERDINAND is discovered occupied in a meaningless task—moving logs from
one pile to another. MIRANDA enters and tries to convince him to rest. As
MIRANDA enters, so does PROSPERO, unseen by the two lovers. FERDINAND
and MIRANDA declare their affection for one another while PROSPERO watch-
es approvingly. Throughout the scene, it is unclear whether or not PROSPERO
can hear exactly what it is the two young lovers are saying because much of
their dialogue is overladen with sexual subtext. In essence, MIRANDA and
FERDINAND are flirting shamelessly with each other. At the end of the scene,
the lovers are left engaged to be married and PROSPERO leaves to continue his
plan with the other courtiers on the island.

---

382  *him*  Possibly referring to the bottle or to Caliban.
383  *dams*  A method of catching fish by damming streams.
384  *at requiring*  On demand.
385  *trencher*  A flat piece of wood on which meat was served. Servants would scrape the leftovers
off of their lord's trenchers for their own meals.
386  *hey-day*  High-day, holy day, or holiday.
387  *brave*  Sarcastically said.

## Act Three
## Scene One

*Enter FERDINAND, bearing a log.*

**Ferdinand** There be some sports[388] are painful, and their labour
    Delight in them sets off. Some kinds of baseness
    Are nobly undergone[389] and most poor matters
    Point to rich ends. This my mean[390] task
    Would be as heavy[391] to me as odious, but            5
    The mistress which I serve quickens what's dead
    And makes my labours pleasures: O, she is
    Ten times more gentle than her father's crabbed,[392]
    And he's composed of harshness.[393] I must remove
    Some thousands of these logs and pile them up,       10
    Upon a sore injunction.[394] My sweet mistress
    Weeps when she sees me work, and says such baseness
    Had never like executor. I forget.
    But these sweet thoughts do even refresh my labours
    Most busilest[395] when I do it.

*Enter MIRANDA and PROSPERO. [PROSPERO is at a distance, unseen.]*

**Miranda**                 Alas, now, pray you,       15
    Work not so hard. I would the lightning had
    Burnt up those logs that you are enjoined to pile!
    Pray set it down, and rest you. When this burns,
    'Twill weep[396] for having wearied you. My father

---

388  *sports*  Any exercises or athletic entertainments, hence carrying logs. Sport in the Shakespearean sense could also mean a general diversion, pastime, or amusement, more frequently associated with pleasure than pain, as it is here.

389  *Some kinds . . . undergone*  One may do base or servile acts and still maintain the dignity of nobility.

390  *mean*  Humble.

391  *heavy*  Schmidt notes how this word has different significations that are barely distinguishable and give rise to much quibbling. The general sense of the word is associated with being a weighty or ponderous matter, something not borne easily, something oppressive, tiresome, or annoying. Alexander Schmidt, *Shakespeare Lexicon and Quotation Dictionary*, vol. 1 (Berlin: Reimer, 1902), 528.

392  *crabbed*  Unpleasant, crabby.

393  *harshness*  Severity.

394  *injunction*  Command.

395  *busilest*  A unique superlative form of "busily." Ferdinand is saying that he thinks of Miranda most when he is working.

396  *'Twill weep*  Sap bleeds from a burning log.

The world-renowned circus company Cirque du Soleil, based out of Montreal and founded in 1984 by two Québécois, Guy Laliberté and Gilles Ste-Croix, staged *Amaluna* in 2012, a very loose adaptation of *The Tempest* featuring an example of gender play. Top: Marie-Michelle Faber (Moon Goddess); bottom: Iuliia Mykhailova (Miranda) in *Amaluna*, Cirque du Soleil, directed by Diane Paulus. Photo: Yanick Déry. Costume: Mérédith Caron. © 2012 Cirque du Soleil.

David Garneau, *Riel/Caliban*, 2003. Used by permission of Daniel Fischlin. Photograph: Daniel Fischlin.

Is hard at study. Pray now, rest yourself.                                    20
He's safe[397] for these three hours.
**Ferdinand**                              O most dear mistress,
   The sun will set before I shall discharge
   What I must strive to do.
**Miranda**                         If you'll sit down,
   I'll bear your logs the while. Pray, give me that;
   I'll carry it to the pile.
**Ferdinand**                      No, precious creature,          25
   I had rather crack my sinews,[398] break my back,
   Than you should such dishonour undergo
   While I sit lazy by.
**Miranda**               It would become me
   As well as it does you, and I should do it
   With much more ease, for my good will is to it,          30
   And yours it is against.
**Prospero** [*Aside.*]
                       Poor worm,[399] thou art infected!
   This visitation shows it.
**Miranda**                    You look wearily.
**Ferdinand**  No, noble mistress, 'tis fresh morning with me
   When you are by at night. I do beseech you—
   Chiefly that I might set it in my prayers—          35
   What is your name?
**Miranda**                 Miranda—O my father,
   I have broke your hest[400] to say so.
**Ferdinand**                      Admired Miranda![401]
   Indeed the top of admiration, worth
   What's dearest[402] to the world! Full many a lady

---

397   *safe*  Safely busy.
398   *crack my sinews*  Sprain my tendons.
399   *worm*  A macabre image used to describe love as a kind of infection. "Poor worm" was a
   common enough expression of pity in Shakespeare's time.
400   *hest*  Command, bidding.
401   *Admired Miranda*  Punning on her name. Though Miranda's name derives from the Latin
   word *mirandus*, meaning that which is to be wondered or marvelled at, it is useful to point
   out how close it is etymologically to the Spanish word *mirando*, the present participle of the
   verb *mirar*, meaning "to watch"—thus "watching." The two potential senses play on Miranda
   as the object of Ferdinand's gaze but also of the shipwrecked courtiers as the objects of
   Miranda's watchful eyes.
402   *dearest*  Most valuable.

I have eyed with best regard and many a time 40
Th' harmony of their tongues hath into bondage
Brought my too diligent[403] ear. For several virtues
Have I liked several women; never any
With so full soul, but some defect in her
Did quarrel with the noblest grace she owed[404] 45
And put it to the foil.[405] But you, O you,
So perfect and so peerless, are created
Of every creature's best.

**Miranda**                    I do not know
One of my sex, no woman's face remember,
Save from my glass, mine own. Nor have I seen 50
More that I may call men than you, good friend,
And my dear father. How features are abroad,
I am skilless[406] of, but by my modesty,[407]
The jewel in my dower,[408] I would not wish
Any companion in the world but you, 55
Nor can imagination form a shape,
Besides yourself, to like of. But I prattle
Something too wildly and my father's precepts
I therein do forget.

**Ferdinand**                    I am, in my condition,[409]
A prince, Miranda; I do think, a king— 60
I would not so![410]—and would no more endure
This wooden slavery than to suffer
The flesh-fly blow[411] my mouth. Hear my soul speak:
The very instant that I saw you, did
My heart fly to your service, there resides 65
To make me slave to it, and for your sake
Am I this patient log-man.

---

403 *diligent* Attentive.
404 *owed* Owned.
405 *foil* Ferdinand is drawing on fencing imagery. All the women he has known had some defect that spoiled their virtues.
406 *skilless* Ignorant, inexpert. To possess skill was to have wit, cunning, discernment, ability, and knowledge of the arts and sciences that had practical application.
407. *modesty* Virginity.
408 *dower* Dowry.
409 *condition* Rank, position.
410 *would not so* Wish it were not so.
411 *blow* Lay eggs in; also, to pollute or corrupt. A fly will lay eggs in sores and wounds, thus the image is a particularly gruesome one.

**Miranda**                      Do you love me?

**Ferdinand**  O heaven, O earth, bear witness to this sound

And crown what I profess with kind event[412]

If I speak true; if hollowly, invert                                              70

What best is boded me to mischief![413] I,

Beyond all limit of what[414] else i' th' world

Do love, prize, honour you.

**Miranda**                             I am a fool

To weep at what I am glad of.

**Prospero** [*Aside.*]

                                   Fair encounter

Of two most rare affections! Heavens rain grace                    75

On that which breeds between 'em!

**Ferdinand**                         Wherefore weep you?

**Miranda**  At mine unworthiness, that dare not offer

What I desire to give, and much less take

What I shall die to want. But this is trifling,[415]

And all the more it seeks to hide itself,                                     80

The bigger bulk it shows.[416] Hence, bashful cunning,[417]

And prompt me, plain and holy innocence!

I am your wife, if you will marry me—

If not, I'll die your maid.[418] To be your fellow[419]

---

412  *kind event*  Good fortune.

413  *If hollowly . . . mischief*  Turn the happiness that I am promised to mischance if I lie.

414  *what*  Whatever.

415  *At mine . . . trifling*  There are at least two readings at play here. Stevenson provides the more romantic or idealistic reading by glossing Miranda as saying that she "dare not offer my love, much less, accept yours" (Stevenson, *The Tempest*, 102). The alternate, sexual meaning hinges on "die," which was a euphemism for "orgasm" in Shakespeare's day. Thus, she is also saying that she dare not offer her body (what she desires to give), nor take (in the sense of "taking in") what she needs (what she wants or lacks) to achieve orgasm. In short, she is flirting with Ferdinand as, at the beginning of the next sentence, she describes the sexual innuendo as "trifling." That word can mean cheating (in the sense she is playing the game of seduction better than him), but also joking in order to amuse, and talking frivolously.

416  *The bigger . . . shows*  The reference is to an attempt to hide a pregnancy.

417  *bashful cunning*  False innocence, with a secondary implication recognizing the sexual double meaning of the previous lines.

418  *maid*  Virgin, also servant.

419  *your fellow*  Two senses of "fellow" are at play here. On the one hand, the term can mean "mate" or "spouse," which seems the primary meaning. "Fellow" also meant "partner" or "equal," and was used to refer to women in the period (*OED*, 3rd ed., s.v. "fellow," n1c). If this secondary meaning is at play, then "servant" may, in turn, refer to "mate." As with all Shakespeare, all meanings are probably at play without the exclusion of any single meaning.

You may deny me, but I'll be your servant,                                              85
Whether you will or no.
**Ferdinand**                          My mistress,[420] dearest,
And I thus humble ever.

[*He kneels.*]

**Miranda**  My husband, then?
**Ferdinand**                          Aye, with a heart as willing
As bondage e'er of freedom. Here's my hand.
**Miranda**  And mine, with my heart in't. And now farewell              90
Till half an hour hence.
**Ferdinand**                          A thousand thousand![421]

*Exeunt* [FERDINAND *and* MIRANDA.]

**Prospero**  So glad of this as they I cannot be,
Who are surprised withal,[422] but my rejoicing
At nothing can be more. I'll to my book,
For yet ere supper-time must I perform                                       95
Much business appertaining.[423]

[*Exit.*]

# ACT THREE, SCENE TWO (3.2)

This scene combines a light comic interlude with the dark and sinister actions of murder and usurpation. STEPHANO, TRINCULO, and CALIBAN—all drunk—plan how they will kill PROSPERO and take over the island. As CALIBAN begins to explain the plan, ARIEL enters, invisible. In order to confound their plans, ARIEL imitates the voices of the conspirators, sowing dissent in the group and providing a moment of slapstick violence. STEPHANO orders TRINCULO to stand back as CALIBAN explains how they should kill PROSPERO and take MIRANDA. Once the plan is explained, ARIEL plays music to the trio to draw them off. They all stagger offstage together, following the sound.

---

420  *mistress*  A woman who commands a man, with no suggestion of illicit or extramarital affairs.
421  *thousand thousand*  A million (goodbyes).
422  *withal*  By it.
423  *business appertaining*  Tasks that are to do, related work.

## Act Three
## Scene Two

*Enter CALIBAN, STEPHANO, and TRINCULO.*

**Stephano**  Tell not me.[424] When the butt is out,[425] we will drink water; not a
   drop before. Therefore bear up, and board 'em.[426] Servant monster, drink
   to me.

**Trinculo**  Servant monster! The folly[427] of this island! They say there's but five
   upon this isle: we are three of them. If th' other two be brained[428] like us,     5
   the state totters.

**Stephano**  Drink, servant monster, when I bid thee. Thy eyes are almost set[429] in
   thy head.

**Trinculo**  Where should they be set else? He were a brave[430] monster indeed, if
   they were set in his tail.     10

**Stephano**  My man monster hath drowned his tongue in sack. For my part,
   the sea cannot drown me. I swam, ere I could recover the shore, five and
   thirty leagues off and on. By this light, thou shalt be my lieutenant,
   monster, or my standard.[431]

**Trinculo**  Your lieutenant, if you list;[432] he's no standard.[433]     15

**Stephano**  We'll not run,[434] Monsieur Monster.

**Trinculo**  Nor go neither; but you'll lie like dogs[435] and yet say nothing neither.

**Stephano**  Mooncalf, speak once in thy life, if thou be'st a good mooncalf.

**Caliban**  How does thy honour? Let me lick thy shoe. I'll not serve him; he's not
   valiant.     20

**Trinculo**  Thou liest, most ignorant monster: I am in case to jostle a
   constable.[436] Why, thou debauched fish, thou, was there ever man a coward
   that hath drunk so much sack as I today? Wilt thou tell a monstrous lie,
   being but half a fish and half a monster?

---

424  *Tell not me*  It is possible Trinculo has told Stephano that the supplies of liquor are running low.
425  *out*  Empty.
426  *board 'em*  Drink up.
427  *folly*  This can either refer to Stephano, calling him a kind of fool, or to Caliban, calling him a
   kind of freak.
428  *brained*  Addle-brained or drunk. Also, intending to seize power.
429  *set*  Sunk. Trinculo puns upon the more common meaning of "placed."
430  *brave*  Drunk.
431  *standard*  A flag-bearer, usually put in the vanguard of an army.
432  *list*  Like; also to lean to one side.
433  *no standard*  Cannot stand straight.
434  *run*  From battle.
435  *lie like dogs*  Proverbial: To lie (in the fields) like dogs. Also, a pun on the word "lie," meaning
   to not tell the truth. See Tilley, *Dictionary of Proverbs*, D435, D529.
436  *I am . . . constable*  I am in a state (I am so drunk) that I would fight a policeman.

*Caliban* Lo, how he mocks me! Wilt thou let him, my lord?                    25

*Trinculo* "Lord," quoth he! That a monster should be such a natural!⁴³⁷

*Caliban* Lo, lo, again! Bite him to death, I prithee.

*Stephano* Trinculo, keep a good tongue in your head.⁴³⁸ If you prove a
mutineer, the next tree!⁴³⁹ The poor monster's my subject and he shall not
suffer indignity.                                                            30

*Caliban* I thank my noble lord. Wilt thou be pleased to hearken once again to
the suit I made to thee?

*Stephano* Marry, will I. Kneel and repeat it. I will stand, and so shall Trinculo.

*Enter ARIEL, invisible.*

*Caliban* As I told thee before, I am subject to a tyrant,
A sorcerer, that by his cunning hath                                         35
Cheated me of the island.

*Ariel* Thou liest.⁴⁴⁰

*Caliban* [*To TRINCULO.*]
                    Thou liest, thou jesting monkey, thou!
I would my valiant master would destroy thee!
I do not lie.

*Stephano* Trinculo, if you trouble him any more in's tale, by this hand, I will   40
supplant some of your teeth.

*Trinculo* Why, I said nothing.

*Stephano* Mum, then, and no more. Proceed.

*Caliban* I say by sorcery he got this isle.
From me he got it. If thy greatness will                                     45
Revenge it on him—for I know thou dar'st,
But this thing dare not—

*Stephano* That's most certain.

*Caliban* Thou shalt be lord of it, and I'll serve thee.

*Stephano* How now shall this be compassed?⁴⁴¹                               50
Canst thou bring me to the party?

*Caliban* Yea, yea, my lord. I'll yield him thee asleep,
Where thou may'st knock a nail into his head.

---

437  *natural*  A natural fool was one born with mental incapacity.

438  *keep a . . . head*  Proverbial: "Mind what you say."

439  *mutineer . . . tree*  Army mutineers were hung from available trees.

440  *Thou liest*  Elsewhere in the canon, Shakespeare presents a spirit imitating the voice of a human for comic effect. See *A Midsummer Night's Dream* 3.2.360–61.

441  *compassed*  Accomplished; to "compass" has multiple meanings including to encircle, to possess, and to bring about or to effect something. It is probably intended in this latter sense by Stephano.

**Ariel** Thou liest; thou canst not.

**Caliban** What a pied ninny's this!⁴⁴² Thou scurvy patch!⁴⁴³      55
    I do beseech thy greatness, give him blows
    And take his bottle from him. When that's gone
    He shall drink naught but brine,⁴⁴⁴ for I'll not show him
    Where the quick freshes are.

**Stephano** Trinculo, run into no further danger. Interrupt the monster one    60
    word further, and, by this hand, I'll turn my mercy out o' doors and make a
    stockfish⁴⁴⁵ of thee.

**Trinculo** Why, what did I? I did nothing. I'll go farther off.

**Stephano** Did'st thou not say he lied?

**Ariel** Thou liest.      65

**Stephano** Do I so? Take thou that.

    [*Beats TRINCULO.*]

    As you like this, give me the lie another time!

**Trinculo** I did not give the lie! Out o' your wits and hearing too? A pox⁴⁴⁶
    o' your bottle!
    This can sack and drinking do. A murrain⁴⁴⁷ on your monster, and the devil   70
    take your fingers!

**Caliban** Ha, ha, ha!

**Stephano** Now, forward with your tale. [*To TRINCULO.*]
    Prithee, stand farther off.

**Caliban** Beat him enough. After a little time      75
    I'll beat him too.

**Stephano** Stand farther. Come, proceed.

**Caliban** Why, as I told thee, 'tis a custom with him,
    I' th' afternoon to sleep. There thou may'st brain him,
    Having first seized his books; or with a log      80
    Batter his skull, or paunch⁴⁴⁸ him with a stake,
    Or cut his wezand⁴⁴⁹ with thy knife. Remember

---

442  *pied ninny*  "Pied" refers to the multicoloured cloak worn by fools. "Ninny" refers to the fool.

443  *scurvy patch*  Another term for contemptible fool.

444  *brine*  Salt water.

445  *stockfish*  Dried or salted cod used to create broth or stock. The joke comes from the prepa-
    ration method, which involved beating the fish and rubbing it with salt.

446  *pox*  Here, a generalized curse. Often "pox" refers specifically to syphilis, a sexually transmit-
    ted disease.

447  *murrain*  A disease or plague.

447  *paunch*  To stab in the paunch (the stomach).

448  *wezand*  Windpipe.

449  *sot*  Drunkard, though here the meaning seems to be something more akin to "fool."

First to possess his books; for without them
He's but a sot,[450] as I am, nor hath not
One spirit to command—they all do hate him                    85
As rootedly as I. Burn but his books.
He has brave utensils, for so he calls them,
Which when he has a house, he'll deck withal.
And that most deeply to consider is
The beauty of his daughter. He himself                         90
Calls her a nonpareil.[451] I never saw a woman,
But only Sycorax my dam[452] and she;
But she as far surpasseth Sycorax
As great'st does least.

**Stephano**               Is it so brave a lass?

**Caliban**  Aye, lord, she will become thy bed, I warrant,     95
And bring thee forth brave brood.

**Stephano**  Monster, I will kill this man. His daughter and I will be king and
queen—save our graces—and Trinculo and thyself shall be viceroys.[453]
Dost thou like the plot, Trinculo?

**Trinculo**  Excellent.                                             100

**Stephano**  Give me thy hand. I am sorry I beat thee. But while thou livest, keep
a good tongue in thy head.

**Caliban**  Within this half hour will he be asleep.
Wilt thou destroy him then?

**Stephano**               Aye, on mine honour.

**Ariel**  This will I tell my master.                                 105

**Caliban**  Thou mak'st me merry; I am full of pleasure.
Let us be jocund.[454] Will you troll the catch[455]
You taught me but whilere?[456]

**Stephano**  At thy request, monster. I will do reason, any reason.
Come on, Trinculo, let us sing.                                 110

*Sings.*

---

450  *nonpareil*  French phrase for a person without equal.
451  *dam*  Mother.
452  *viceroys*  A viceroy was a noble appointed to rule in the place of the monarch during an
absence or a minority.
454  *jocund*  Happy, merry.
455  *troll the catch*  A catch was a song sung in the round (a modern example would be the nurs-
ery rhyme "Row, Row, Row Your Boat"). The catch could be sung by any number of voices,
though three or four was common practice. Catches would have been regular features of pubs
and popular entertainment. To troll was to warble or to sing happily.
456  *whilere*  Just now.

> Flout 'em and scout[457] 'em
> And scout 'em and flout 'em
> Thought is free.

**Caliban**  That's not the tune.

*Ariel plays the tune on a tabor[458] and pipe.*

**Stephano**  What is this same?                                      115
**Trinculo**  This is the tune of our catch, played by the picture of Nobody.[459]
**Stephano**  If thou be'st a man, show thyself in thy likeness. If thou be'st a devil, take't as thou list.[460]
**Trinculo**  O, forgive me my sins!
**Stephano**  He that dies pays all debts.[461] I defy thee. Mercy upon us!   120
**Caliban**  Art thou afeard?
**Stephano**  No monster, not I.
**Caliban**  Be not afeard, the isle is full of noises,
Sounds, and sweet airs, that give delight and hurt not.
Sometimes a thousand twangling instruments             125
Will hum about mine ears; and sometime voices
That if I then had waked after long sleep,
Will make me sleep again, and then, in dreaming,
The clouds, methought, would open and show riches
Ready to drop upon me, that when I waked,               130
I cried to dream again.
**Stephano**  This will prove a brave kingdom to me, where I shall have my music for nothing.
**Caliban**  When Prospero is destroyed.
**Stephano**  That shall be by and by. I remember the story.      135
**Trinculo**  The sound is going away. Let's follow it, and after do our work.
**Stephano**  Lead, monster; we'll follow. I would I could see this taborer; he lays it on.
**Trinculo**  [*To CALIBAN.*]
Wilt come? I'll follow, Stephano.

*[Exeunt.]*

---

457  *scout*  To mock.
458  *tabor*  A small drum.
459  *picture of Nobody*  "The reference is probably to the pictures that were common on the sign-boards showing a head and shoulders but no distinct features on the face" (Stevenson, *The Tempest*, 104).
460  *If thou . . . list*  Proverbial. "Take as you will." That is, Stephano is saying that if the spirit is a devil, they cannot stop him from doing whatever he wishes.
461  *He that . . . debts*  Proverbial. "Death pays all debts" (Tilley, *Dictionary of Proverbs*, D148).

# ACT THREE, SCENE THREE (3.3)

This scene is a preparation for the *coup de théâtre* that is the masque scene in act four. Here, the special effects of the disappearing banquet would have amazed theatregoers of the seventeenth century. The court of the King of Naples comes on stage. ALONSO is still despondent and SEBASTIAN and ANTONIO are still planning the death of the king.

PROSPERO enters invisibly and magically calls forth a banquet before the Neapolitan courtiers. They debate whether they should eat from the banquet until ALONSO orders them to do so, having despaired that his life will ever be any better. When ALONSO orders the courtiers to eat, ARIEL appears dressed as a harpy, a mythical half-woman, half-bird creature that ate human flesh. ARIEL reprimands the courtiers for having, once upon a time, overthrown PROSPERO, and says that their presence on the island is a just punishment for them. In a flash of thunder and lightning, the banquet and ARIEL both disappear.

ALONSO, ANTONIO, and SEBASTIAN are driven wild by the sight of ARIEL and while the two traitors run off to seek more devils, ALONSO flies in despair of his complicity in the apparent murder of PROSPERO years before. GONZALO follows the others, fearing for their safety.

### Act Three
### Scene Three

*Enter ALONSO, SEBASTIAN, ANTONIO, GONZALO, ADRIAN, FRANCISCO, and others.*

**Gonzalo** [*To ALONSO.*]
By'r lakin,[462] I can go no further, sir,
My old bones ache. Here's a maze trod indeed
Through forth-rights[463] and meanders! By your patience,
I needs must rest me.

**Alonso**                    Old lord, I cannot blame thee,
Who am myself attached[464] with weariness,                    5
To th' dulling of my spirits. Sit down and rest.
Even here I will put off my hope, and keep it

---

462  *lakin*  Short form for "ladykin," a term for the Virgin Mary.
463  *forth-rights*  Straight paths.
464  *attached*  Seized.

No longer for[465] my flatterer. He is drowned
Whom thus we stray to find, and the sea mocks
Our frustrate search on land. Well, let him go.                    10
**Antonio** [*Aside to SEBASTIAN.*]
I am right glad that he's so out of hope.
Do not for one repulse forego the purpose
That you resolved t'effect.
**Sebastian** [*Aside to ANTONIO.*]
                                        The next advantage
Will we take throughly.[466]
**Antonio** [*Aside to SEBASTIAN.*]
                                        Let it be tonight,
For now they are oppressed with travail;[467] they                15
Will not nor cannot use such vigilance
As when they are fresh.
**Sebastian** [*Aside to ANTONIO.*]
            I say tonight. No more.

*Solemn and strange music.*

**Alonso**  What harmony is this? My good friends, hark!
**Gonzalo**  Marvellous sweet music!                              20

*Enter PROSPERO above, invisible. Enter several strange shapes bringing in
a banquet. They dance about it with gentle actions of salutation, and inviting
the king, etc., to eat, they depart.*

**Alonso**  Give us kind keepers,[468] heavens! What were these?
**Sebastian**  A living drollery![469] Now I will believe
That there are unicorns; that in Arabia
There is one tree, the phoenix' throne, one phoenix
At this hour reigning there.[470]

---

465  *for*  As.
466  *throughly*  Thoroughly.
467  *travail*  Both physical labour, toil, exertion, and travelling or journeying. Intriguingly, the word
      also denoted a heavenly eclipse in Shakespeare's day (*OED*, 3rd ed., s.v. "travail," n1, def. 5),
      which may connect with the "auspicious star" that Prospero mentions in act one.
468  *kind keepers*  Guardian angels.
469  *A living drollery*  Puppet show with live actors.
470  *phoenix' throne . . . there*  The myth of the phoenix was popular throughout the Middle
      Ages and Renaissance for the perceived similarities between it and Christ. Only one phoenix
      existed at a time, and it supposedly lived in Arabia. At the end of its life, it created a funeral
      pyre (the "throne") that was ignited by the sun. The phoenix burned upon the pyre and from
      the ashes appeared an egg, from which a new phoenix appeared.

**Antonio**                                  I'll believe both;                    25
And what does else want credit,[471] come to me,
And I'll be sworn 'tis true. Travellers ne'er did lie,
Though fools at home condemn 'em.

**Gonzalo**                                  If in Naples
I should report this now, would they believe me?
If I should say, I saw such islanders—                               30
For certes,[472] these are people of the island—
Who, though they are of monstrous[473] shape, yet, note,
Their manners are more gentle-kind than of
Our human generation you shall find
Many, nay, almost any.

**Prospero**  [*Aside.*]
                                  Honest lord,                        35
Thou hast said well, for some of you there present
Are worse than devils.[474]

**Alonso**                        I cannot too much muse[475]
Such shapes, such gesture, and such sound, expressing—
Although they want the use of tongue—a kind
Of excellent dumb discourse.

**Prospero**  [*Aside.*]
                                  Praise in departing.[476]            40

**Francisco**  They vanished strangely.

**Sebastian**                        No matter, since
They have left their viands[477] behind; for we have stomachs.[478]
Will't please you taste of what is here?

**Alonso**                                  Not I.

**Gonzalo**  Faith, sir, you need not fear. When we were boys,
Who would believe that there were mountaineers                        45

---

471  *want credit*  Lack credence.
472  *For certes*  For sure, certainly.
473  *monstrous*  Unnatural.
474  *for some . . . devils*  Though we think of this as a comedy, we must remember that when this
     was first performed, no one would know what Prospero would do with his brother. Here, he
     clearly has not forgiven him. Shakespeare drops hints throughout the play that undercut the
     image of Prospero as a kindly old man, including in act five stating outright that Prospero is a
     necromancer. What Prospero will do in act five should not be a foregone conclusion. Where
     else in the play does Shakespeare present Prospero in a dark or unflattering light?
475  *muse*  Wonder at.
476  *Praise in departing*  Wait until the conclusion before you give me praise.
477  *viands*  Foodstuffs.
478  *stomachs*  Appetites.

Dewlapped[479] like bulls, whose throats had hanging at 'em
Wallets of flesh?—or that there were such men
Whose heads stood in their breasts?[480]—which now we find
Each putter-out of five for one[481] will bring us
Good warrant of.

**Alonso**                          I will stand to[482] and feed,                          50
Although my last—no matter, since I feel
The best[483] is past. Brother, my lord the duke,
Stand to and do as we.

*Thunder and lightning.*

*Enter ARIEL, like a harpy.*[484] *[He] claps his wings upon the table and,*
*with a quaint device,*[485] *the banquet vanishes.*

**Ariel**  You are three men of sin, whom Destiny,
That hath to instrument this lower world                          55
And what is in't, the never-surfeited sea[486]
Hath caused to belch up you, and on this island
Where man doth not inhabit—you 'mongst men
Being most unfit to live—I have made you mad;
And even with such-like valour[487] men hang and drown                          60
Their proper[488] selves.

---

471  *want credit*  Lack credence.
480  *that there . . . breasts*  Travel literature of the period was filled with such stories. For example, despite the dominance of the Songhai empire for the two hundred years previous to the time of Shakespeare, the strength of the Ethiopian Empire, and the overwhelming efficiency of Arab administration north of the Sahara, Africa as a whole, and its inhabitants in particular, were always described in these travel narratives as chaotic. Likewise, travel narratives of North America and elsewhere described tribes of indigenous peoples whose bodies were missing limbs or who had extra limbs.
481  *putter-out of . . . one*  A reference to a kind of early travel insurance. When an expedition left England, a traveller would put down money with an insurer and, if they returned with proof that they had reached their destination, they would receive five times the amount they had put down. Given the dangers of transatlantic travel at the time, the business was a profitable one for insurers.
482  *stand to*  Risk it.
483  *best*  Best part of my life.
484  *harpy*  A winged monster from Greek myth, with the face and body of a woman and a bird of prey's claws.
485  *quaint device*  Ingenious stage mechanism. This section, like the masque in act four with the spirits as goddesses, was spectacular and made the most of the possibilities of theatrical illusion and stagecraft.
486  *never-surfeited sea*  The hungry sea. "Surfeit" indicated the range of emotions, from satisfaction to disgust, arising from excessive consumption.
487  *such-like valour*  The courage of the mad (not true courage).
488  *proper*  Own.

[*ANTONIO and SEBASTIAN draw their swords.*[489]]

              You fools! I and my fellows
Are ministers of Fate. The elements
Of whom[490] your swords are tempered, may as well
Wound the loud winds, or with bemocked-at[491] stabs
Kill the still-closing waters, as diminish              65
One dowl[492] that's in my plume. My fellow ministers
Are like invulnerable. If you could hurt,
Your swords are now too massy for your strengths,
And will not be uplifted. But remember—
For that's my business to you—that you three          70
From Milan did supplant good Prospero,
Exposed unto the sea, which hath requit it,[493]
Him and his innocent child; for which foul deed
The powers, delaying, not forgetting, have
Incensed the seas and shores—yea, all the creatures—    75
Against your peace. Thee of thy son, Alonso,
They have bereft, and do pronounce by me
Ling'ring perdition,[494] worse than any death
Can be at once, shall step by step attend
You and your ways, whose wraths to guard you from—    80
Which here, in this most desolate isle, else falls
Upon your heads—is nothing but heart's sorrow,[495]
And a clear life ensuing.[496]

*He vanishes in thunder. Then, to soft music enter the shapes again, and dance, with mocks and mows,[497] and carrying out the table.*

---

489  ANTONIO and . . . swords  Only Antonio and Sebastian are indicated in this edition as drawing their weapons, but all of the courtiers could very well have drawn their swords at this point. The internal stage direction only indicates that multiple swords are drawn, not who draws them.
490  *whom*  Which.
491  *bemocked-at*  Fruitless, ridiculous.
492  *dowl*  Feather.
493  *requit it*  Repaid the act.
494  *Ling'ring perdition*  Everlasting hellfire. Perdition means destruction, ruin, and loss.
495  *is nothing . . . sorrow*  There is no means but repentance.
496  *ensuing*  Hereafter.
497  *mocks and mows*  Mocking gestures and facial expressions.

*Prospero* Bravely[498] the figure of this harpy hast thou
    Performed, my Ariel; a grace it had, devouring.[499]        85
    Of my instruction hast thou nothing bated[500]
    In what thou hadst to say. So with good life
    And observation strange, my meaner ministers
    Their several kinds have done.[501] My high charms work,
    And these mine enemies are all knit up        90
    In their distractions.[502] They now are in my power;
    And in these fits I leave them, while I visit
    Young Ferdinand, whom they suppose is drowned,
    And his and mine loved darling.

                                          *[Exit.]*

*Gonzalo* I' th' name of something holy, sir, why stand you    95
    In this strange stare?
*Alonso*                O, it is monstrous, monstrous!
    Methought the billows spoke and told me of it,
    The winds did sing it to me; and the thunder,
    That deep and dreadful organ-pipe, pronounced
    The name of Prosper. It did bass my trespass.[503]    100
    Therefore my son i' th' ooze is bedded, and
    I'll seek him deeper than e'er plummet[504] sounded
    And with him there lie mudded.

                                          *[Exit.]*

*Sebastian*                  But one fiend at a time,
    I'll fight their legions o'er.[505]
*Antonio*               I'll be thy second.[506]

                      *Exeunt [SEBASTIAN and ANTONIO.]*

---

498  *Bravely* Splendidly, excellently.
499  *devouring* Both a "ravishing grace" and an indication that the banquet disappeared
      gracefully.
500  *bated* Omitted.
501  *So with . . . done* "So, also, my humbler agents have performed their respective duties most
      naturally and with wonderful fidelity to my instructions" (Stevenson, *The Tempest*, 107).
502  *knit up . . . distractions* Tangled in confusions.
503  *bass my trespass* To sound, but also a pun on the baseness of the action.
504  *plummet* Weight attached to the end of a rope, which sailors use to test water depth.
505  *But one . . . o'er* Even if the devils come one at a time, I'll fight them all.
506  *second* A backup or auxiliary combatant in a duel.

**Gonzalo** All three of them are desperate: their great guilt, 105
    Like poison given to work a great time after,
    Now 'gins[507] to bite the spirits. I do beseech you
    That are of suppler joints, follow them swiftly
    And hinder them from what this ecstasy[508]
    May now provoke them to. 110
**Adrian** Follow, I pray you.

*[Exeunt omnes.]*

# ACT FOUR, SCENE ONE (4.1)

This scene is a kind of masque in miniature. The masque was a uniquely Renaissance dramatic form, very expensive to mount and performed for royalty and aristocracy, where spectacle, allegory, and audience participation were all expected. Here, the emphasis is on spectacle, yet the stage directions can only hint at what we might have seen in Shakespeare's day. We discover FERDINAND and MIRANDA with PROSPERO, who blesses the marriage of the two young lovers, yet delivers a hyperbolic threat regarding chastity at the same time. ARIEL enters and PROSPERO orders him to bring the other spirits and put on a spectacle for the young couple.

PROSPERO orders FERDINAND and MIRANDA to watch as IRIS, CERES, and JUNO descend and pronounce their blessings on the upcoming marriage. The focus at this point is on spectacular visuals and poetic music rather than action onstage. In terms of action for the plot, very little happens in this sequence other than that the goddesses grant their blessings upon the upcoming marriage. Then, Reapers and Nymphs appear on stage and dance in celebration.

PROSPERO interrupts the spectacle when he remembers the conspiracy of CALIBAN, TRINCULO, and STEPHANO. He comforts FERDINAND and MIRANDA with one of the most famous speeches in Shakespeare's entire canon and then sends the lovers away. PROSPERO then orders ARIEL to bring the drunken trio to him. ARIEL exits and returns with his arms filled with beautiful clothes, which he scatters about the stage.

---

507 *'gins* Begins.
508 *ecstasy* Madness. Ecstasy generally referenced any state of being beside one's self, ranging from violent passion to extreme disquietude. It could also mean a fainting fit or swoon.

CALIBAN and the others appear while PROSPERO and ARIEL are invisible. STEPHANO and TRINCULO, seeing the clothing, become distracted from their purpose, which CALIBAN insists is the murder of PROSPERO. They fight over the clothes and their mission for a while.

Finally, PROSPERO and ARIEL let loose magical spirits in the shapes of dogs upon CALIBAN, STEPHANO, and TRINCULO and chase them from the stage.

## Act Four
## Scene One

*Enter PROSPERO, FERDINAND, and MIRANDA.*

**Prospero**  If I have too austerely punished you,
Your compensation makes amends, for I
Have given you here a third of mine own life,[509]
Or that for which I live, who once again
I tender to thy hand. All thy vexations                          5
Were but my trials of thy love, and thou
Hast strangely[510] stood the test. Here, afore Heaven,
I ratify this my rich gift. O Ferdinand,
Do not smile at me that I boast her off,[511]
For thou shalt find she will outstrip all praise,               10
And make it halt[512] behind her.
**Ferdinand**                         I do believe it
Against an oracle.[513]
**Prospero**  Then as my gift, and thine own acquisition
Worthily purchased, take my daughter. But
If thou dost break her virgin-knot[514] before                  15

---

509  *a third . . . life*  A number of explanations of this line are possible: first, Prospero has spent a third of his life educating and raising Miranda; second, Miranda is, along with his art and his dukedom, one of Prospero's three riches; and third, Miranda represents his future, while his present and past are the other two parts of his life.

510  *strangely*  Admirably; also, unusually, strangely. Did Prospero expect Ferdinand to stand the test?

511  *boast her off*  Praise her so highly.

512  *halt*  Limp. Miranda is so beyond praise, praise itself limps behind her.

513  *Against an oracle*  Even if an oracle should counter it. An oracle was a medium through whom the will of the gods was made apparent to humans. Christians adopted the concept in terms of the idea of divine revelation of God's will. Ferdinand is hyperbolically saying that he will believe Prospero before he believes any evidence offered against him.

514  *virgin-knot*  Maidenhead, hymen. In classical Rome, Hymen was also the name of the God of Marriage (see below).

All sanctimonious[515] ceremonies may
With full and holy rite be ministered,
No sweet aspersion[516] shall the heavens let fall
To make this contract grow; but barren hate,
Sour-eyed disdain and discord shall bestrew                           20
The union of your bed with weeds so loathly
That you shall hate it both. Therefore take heed,
As Hymen's lamps[517] shall light you.[518]

**Ferdinand**                                            As I hope
For quiet days, fair issue, and long life,
With such love as 'tis now, the murkiest den,                        25
The most opportune place, the strong'st suggestion.[519]
Our worser genius can, shall never melt
Mine honour into lust, to take away
The edge[520] of that day's[521] celebration
When I shall think or Phoebus' steeds are foundered,                 30
Or night kept chained below.[522]

**Prospero**                                            Fairly spoke.
Sit then and talk with her, she is thine own.
What,[523] Ariel! My industrious servant, Ariel!

*Enter ARIEL.*

**Ariel**  What would my potent master? Here I am.
**Prospero**  Thou and thy meaner fellows[524] your last service        35
Did worthily perform, and I must use you

---

515  *sanctimonious*  Holy.
516  *aspersion*  Sprinkling of holy water, here meaning "blessing."
517  *Hymen's lamps*  The Roman God of Marriage who traditionally carried a torch that shone clearly for happy marriages and smoked for unhappy ones.
518  *If thou . . . you*  Prospero launches into a sudden and terrifying threat against Ferdinand, the content of which seems odd and difficult to explain, especially for those critics who try to read Prospero as a stand-in for Shakespeare, and particularly in the context of Anne Hathaway being pregnant when she and Shakespeare wed. If nothing else, this overbearing threat provides insight into the character of Prospero's authoritarian governance of those around him.
519  *suggestion*  Temptation.
520  *edge*  Keenness.
521  *that day's*  The wedding day.
522  *Phoebus' steeds . . . below*  Phoebus was the God of the Sun, who rode through the sky in his chariot. Ferdinand is talking about the wedding day seeming exceedingly long in anticipation of the pleasures of the wedding night.
523  *What*  In this case, an exclamation used to command Ariel's presence.
524  *meaner fellows*  Lesser spirits under Prospero's governance.

In such another trick.[525] Go, bring the rabble[526]—
O'er whom I give thee power—here to this place.
Incite them to quick motion, for I must
Bestow upon the eyes of this young couple                                    40
Some vanity[527] of mine art. It is my promise,
And they expect it from me.
*Ariel*                                        Presently?[528]
*Prospero*  Aye, with a twink.[529]
*Ariel*  Before you can say "come" and "go,"
And breathe twice, and cry "so, so,"                                          45
Each one, tripping[530] on his toe,
Will be here with mop and mow.[531]
Do you love me, master? No?
*Prospero*  Dearly, my delicate Ariel. Do not approach
Till thou dost hear me call.
*Ariel*                                        Well, I conceive.                50

                                                                *Exit.*


*Prospero*  [*To FERDINAND.*]
Look thou be true. Do not give dalliance[532]
Too much the rein.[533] The strongest oaths are straw
To th' fire i' th' blood.[534] Be more abstemious,[535]
Or else good night your vow!
*Ferdinand*                                I warrant you sir;
The white cold virgin snow upon my heart                                      55
Abates the ardour of my liver.[536]
*Prospero*                                Well.
Now come, my Ariel. Bring a corollary,[537]

---

525  *trick*  Ingenious device.
526  *abble*  The lesser spirits.
527  *vanity*  Show, lighthearted display, pageant.
528  *Presently*  Right away?
529  *with a twink*  In the wink of an eye.
530  *tripping*  Moving swiftly, nimbly, gracefully.
531  *mop and mow*  Grimace and gesture.
532  *dalliance*  Idleness or frivolity, but with the additional connotation of sexual flirtation and
     caressing.
533  *Too much . . . rein*  Undue liberty.
534  *The strongest . . . blood*  Sexual desire overpowers even the strongest oaths.
535  *abstemious*  Moderate, temperate, self-governed.
536  *liver*  Where passionate emotions were thought to originate.
537  *corollary*  Extra spirit.

Rather than want[538] a spirit. Appear and pertly![539]
No tongue![540] All eyes! Be silent.

*Soft music.*

*Enter IRIS.*

**Iris**  Ceres, most bounteous lady, thy rich leas[541]                     60
Of wheat, rye, barley, vetches,[542] oats and peas;
Thy turfy[543] mountains, where live nibbling sheep,
And flat meads thatched with stover, them to keep;[544]
Thy banks with pioned and twilled[545] brims,
Which spongy[546] April at thy hest[547] betrims,                            65
To make cold nymphs[548] chaste crowns;[549] and thy broom[550] groves,
Whose shadow the dismissed bachelor[551] loves,
Being lass-lorn;[552] thy pole-clipped vineyard,[553]
And thy sea-marge[554] sterile and rocky-hard,
Where thou thyself dost air—the queen o' th' sky,                           70
Whose watery arch[555] and messenger am I,
Bids thee leave these,[556] and with her sovereign grace,

---

538  *want*  Lack.
539  *pertly*  Promptly.
540  *No tongue*  The charm requires silence from the spectators in order to work, as Prospero indicates later in the scene.
541  *leas*  Meadows, fields.
542  *vetches*  Coarse crops grown primarily for livestock feed.
543  *turfy*  Grass-covered.
544  *flat meads . . . keep*  Meadows covered with hay to keep the sheep through the winter.
545  *pioned and twilled*  Meaning uncertain, but the sense seems to be the banks of a river that have been undercut and undermined by currents of the stream are being reinforced with rushes and roots.
546  *spongy*  Rainy.
547  *hest*  Bidding.
548  *cold nymphs*  Cold because they are chaste virgins.
549  *chaste crowns*  Crowns of flowers, a sign of virginity.
550  *broom*  A kind of shrub with a yellow flower, associated with love spells.
551  *dismissed bachelor*  Rejected male lover.
552  *thy broom . . . lass-lorn*  Shakespeare addresses surprisingly modern issues when you least expect it. The bachelor, or single man, is lass-lorn, or without a woman, thus he likes the broom groves because he can use the herb in a love potion. To put it one way, the bachelor is interested in making an aphrodisiac; to put it another way, he's looking to drug women.
553  *pole-clipped vineyard*  A vineyard hedged in by poles, or a vineyard with poles that have been shortened.
554  *sea-marge*  The margin of the sea.
555  *watery arch*  A rainbow was the traditional symbol of Iris.
556  *these*  The terrain just described.

*JUNO descends.*

Here on this grass-plot, in this very place,
To come and sport. Her peacocks fly amain.[557]
Approach, rich Ceres, her to entertain.                                    75

*Enter CERES.*

**Ceres**  Hail, many-coloured messenger, that ne'er
Dost disobey the wife of Jupiter;[558]
Who with thy saffron wings upon my flowers
Diffusest honey-drops, refreshing showers;
And with each end of thy blue bow dost crown                               80
My bosky[559] acres and my unshrubbed down,[560]
Rich scarf to my proud earth.[561] Why hath thy queen
Summoned me hither, to this short-grassed green?
**Iris**  A contract of true love to celebrate,
And some donation freely to estate[562]                                    85
On the blest lovers.
**Ceres**                            Tell me, heavenly bow,
If Venus or her son,[563] as thou dost know,
Do now attend the Queen? Since they did plot
The means that dusky Dis[564] my daughter got,
Her and her blind boy's scandaled[565] company                            90
I have forsworn.
**Iris**                            Of her society
Be not afraid. I met her deity

---

557  *peacocks fly amain*  Peacocks were birds sacred to Juno in Roman myth, and they pulled her
    chariot. Here they are pulling "amain," that is, with great force or at great speed.
558  *wife of Jupiter*  Juno in Roman myth was the wife of Jupiter.
559  *bosky*  Wooded.
560  *down*  Upland.
561  *My bosky . . . earth*  Shakespeare is drawing on the pastoral tradition of poetry here and, as
    he had done in his early poem *Venus and Adonis*, framing it with an erotic subtext. That is, the
    landscape in pastoral poetry served as an analogue of the eroticized female body, especially
    in poems that celebrated weddings, such as this one does. The image moves down the body
    from "bosky acres" (full head of hair) to "unshrubbed down" (genitals without pubic hair),
    which is the "scarf to [her] proud earth," where "earth" refers to the vagina.
562  *estate*  Bestow.
563  *her son*  Cupid.
564  *Dis*  Pluto, God of the Underworld in Roman myth, who kidnapped and married Ceres's
    daughter Proserpine. The Latin word "*disastra*" or "ill-boding star" (from which our English
    word "*disaster*" comes) descends from the god's name.
565  *scandaled*  Scandalous.

Cutting the clouds towards Paphos,[566] and her son
Dove-drawn[567] with her. Here thought they to have done
Some wanton charm upon this man and maid,                                    95
Whose vows are that no bed-right shall be paid
Till Hymen's torch be lighted, but vain.
Mars's hot minion[568] is returned again;
Her waspish-headed son has broke his arrows,
Swears he will shoot no more, but play with sparrows[569]              100
And be a boy right out.[570]

**Ceres**                                    Highest Queen of state,
Great Juno, comes; I know her by her gait.[571]

*Enter JUNO.*[572]

**Juno**  How does my bounteous sister? Go with me
To bless this twain,[573] that they may prosperous be
And honoured in their issue.                                                    105

*They sing.*

**Juno**      Honour, riches, marriage-blessing,
Long continuance, and increasing,
Hourly joys be still[574] upon you!
Juno sings her blessings upon you.
**Ceres**     Earth's increase, foison[575] plenty,                              110
Barns and garners[576] never empty,
Vines and clustering bunches growing,
Plants with goodly burthen bowing;[577]
Spring come to you at the farthest,

---

566  *Paphos*  A place sacred to Venus, the Roman goddess of love and beauty, in Cyprus.
567  *Dove-drawn*  Venus's chariot was pulled by doves.
568  *hot minion*  Lusty lover; Venus and Mars were lovers.
569  *sparrows*  Proverbially lecherous and sacred to Venus.
570  *right out*  Outright.
571  *gait*  Walk, manner of walking.
572  Enter JUNO  Though the earlier stage direction stated that "JUNO descends," presumably in a stage mechanism made to look like a chariot, here she finally enters the scene. The logistics of her entrance are something every production of *The Tempest* has to deal with.
573  *twain*  Two; Ferdinand and Miranda.
574  *still*  Always.
575  *foison*  Abundance.
576  *garners*  Granaries.
577  *bowing*  Bending.

In the very end of harvest![578]                                         115
Scarcity and want shall shun you;
Ceres' blessing so is on you.

**Ferdinand**  This is a most majestic vision, and
Harmoniously charmingly.[579] May I be bold
To think these spirits?

**Prospero**                    Spirits, which by mine art            120
I have from their confines called to enact
My present fancies.

**Ferdinand**              Let me live here ever!
So rare a wondered[580] father and a wife
Makes this place Paradise.

*JUNO and CERES whisper, and send IRIS on employment.[581]*

**Prospero**                        Sweet, now, silence!
Juno and Ceres whisper seriously.                                      125
There's something else to do. Hush, and be mute,
Or else our spell is marred.

**Iris**  You nymphs, called naiads,[582] of the windering[583] brooks,
With your sedged crowns,[584] and ever-harmless looks,
Leave your crisp channels, and on this green land               130
Answer your summons; Juno does command.
Come, temperate nymphs, and help to celebrate
A contract of true love. Be not too late.

*Enter certain Nymphs.*

---

578  *Spring come . . . harvest*  May Spring come to you as long as possible, even to the end of
harvest. May you have growing weather all year long, in other words.

579  *Harmoniously charmingly*  "The charms are in harmony with one another" (Stevenson, *The
Tempest*, 111).

580  *wondered*  Able to perform such wonders or to be wondered at.

581  *Iris on employment*  Presumably, Iris leaves the stage at this point. Either she returns with the
Reapers and the Nymphs, which is not indicated, or she simply never comes back. It is possible that the Folio text does not have a full description of this portion of the play as it would
have been performed as a masque. Masques were complex, allegorical, often mythological
entertainments that focused on spectacle and were designed to be performed once, before
a royal or noble audience. As we know that this play was performed at the marriage of the
Princess Elizabeth of England to the Elector Palatine of the Holy Roman Empire, it seems
probable that what we have here is a cut version of a larger text wherein Iris returns.

582  *naiads*  Water nymphs.

583  *windering*  Winding and wandering.

584  *sedged crowns*  Crowns woven of sedge, a marsh grass.

You sunburned sickle-men,[585] of August weary,[586]
Come hither from the furrow and be merry;                                     135
Make holiday! Your rye-straw hats put on,
And these fresh nymphs encounter every one
In country footing.[587]

*Enter certain Reapers, properly habited. They join with the Nymphs in a*
*graceful dance, towards the end whereof PROSPERO starts suddenly and*
*speaks, after which, to a strange, hollow, and confused noise, they heavily*
*vanish.*[588]

**Prospero** [*Aside.*]
I had forgot that foul conspiracy
Of the beast Caliban and his confederates                                      140
Against my life. The minute of their plot
Is almost come.

      [*To the Spirits.*]

           Well done! Avoid,[589] no more!

           [*Exeunt JUNO and CERES, Reapers and Nymphs.*]

**Ferdinand** This is strange. Your father's in some passion
   That works[590] him strongly.
**Miranda**                Never till this day
   Saw I him touched with anger so distempered!                               145
**Prospero** [*To FERDINAND.*]
   You do look, my son, in a moved sort,[591]
   As if you were dismayed. Be cheerful, sir;
   Our revels[592] now are ended. These our actors,
   As I foretold you,[593] were all spirits and
   Are melted into air, into thin air,                                        150
   And, like the baseless fabric of this vision,[594]

---

585  *sickle-men*  Harvesters.
586  *of August weary*  Tired of the harvest.
587  *country footing*  A country or rustic dance; also, a country dance was a euphemism for sex.
588  *heavily vanish*  Reluctantly depart, or possibly that they depart through the trap door in the floor.
589  *Avoid*  Begone.
590  *works*  Agitates.
591  *moved sort*  Troubled state.
592  *revels*  Entertainments.
593  *foretold you*  Told you before.
594  *baseless fabric . . . vision*  The spectacle has no material substance.

The cloud-capped towers, the gorgeous palaces,
The solemn temples, the great globe[595] itself,
Yea, all which it inherit,[596] shall dissolve
And, like this insubstantial pageant faded,                    155
Leave not a rack[597] behind. We are such stuff
As dreams are made on,[598] and our little life
Is rounded with[599] a sleep. Sir, I am vexed.
Bear with my weakness, my old brain is troubled.
Be not disturbed with my infirmity.                            160
If you be pleased, retire into my cell,
And there repose. A turn or two I'll walk
To still my beating mind.
**Ferdinand** *and* **Miranda**      We wish your peace.

*Exit* [*MIRANDA and FERDINAND.*]

**Prospero**  Come with a thought![600] I thank thee. Ariel, come!

*Enter ARIEL.*

**Ariel**  Thy thoughts I cleave to.[601] What's thy pleasure?        165
**Prospero**  Spirit, we must prepare to meet with Caliban.
**Ariel**  Aye, my commander. When I presented Ceres,
   I thought to have told thee of it, but I feared
   Lest I might anger thee.
**Prospero**  Say again, where did'st thou leave these varlets?[602]   170
**Ariel**  I told you, sir, they were red-hot with drinking;
   So full of valour that they smote the air
   For breathing in their faces, beat the ground
   For kissing of their feet; yet always bending
   Towards their project.[603] Then I beat my tabor,          175

---

595  *great globe*  The world, but also a possible reference to the Globe Theatre, built in 1599 by Shakespeare's then company, The Lord Chamberlain's Men. It was destroyed by fire on June 29, 1613, then rebuilt in 1614 before it was closed in 1642, as were all theatres when the English Civil War began. A modern reconstruction called "Shakespeare's Globe" opened in 1997 close to the site of the original theatre.
596  *all which . . . inherit*  All the people who live on the earth and who ever will.
597  *rack*  A bank of quick-moving cloud, fog, or sea-spray (*OED* 3rd ed., s.v. "rack," n2, def. 2b).
598  *on*  Of.
599  *rounded with*  Finished by.
500  *with a thought*  As quickly as a thought.
601  *cleave to*  Adhere to.
602  *varlets*  Ruffians, scoundrels.
603  *their project*  Control of the island.

At which, like unbacked[604] colts, they pricked their ears,
Advanced[605] their eyelids, lifted up their noses
As they smelt music. So I charmed their ears
That calf-like they my lowing followed through
Toothed briars, sharp furze's, pricking gorse, and thorns,                    180
Which entered their frail shins. At last I left them
I' th' filthy-mantled[606] pool beyond your cell,
There dancing up to the chins, that the foul lake
O'er-stunk their feet.[607]
**Prospero**                           This was well done, my bird.
Thy shape invisible retain thou still.                                        185
The trumpery[608] in my house, go bring it hither,
For stale[609] to catch these thieves.
**Ariel**                                 I go, I go.

                                                                    [*Exit.*]

**Prospero**   A devil, a born devil, on whose nature
Nurture can never stick; on whom my pains,
Humanely taken—all, all lost, quite lost!                                     190
And, as with age his body uglier grows,
So his mind cankers.[610] I will plague[611] them all,
Even to roaring. Come, hang them on this line.

*Enter ARIEL, loaden with glistering apparel, etc.*

[*PROSPERO and ARIEL remain invisible.*]

*Enter CALIBAN, STEPHANO, and TRINCULO, all wet.*

**Caliban**   Pray you tread softly, that the blind mole[612] may not
Hear a foot fall. We now are near his cell.                                   195
**Stephano**   Monster, your fairy, which you say is a harmless fairy, has done little
better than played the jack[613] with us.

---

604 *unbacked*  Unbroken, wild, not yet ridden.
605 *Advanced*  Lifted.
606 *filthy-mantled*  Covered with scum.
607 *O'er-stunk their feet*  Smelled worse than their feet.
608 *trumpery*  Finery, apparel.
609 *stale*  Bait.
610 *cankers*  Becomes corrupt, malignant.
611 *plague*  Afflict.
612 *blind mole*  Moles were thought to have an exceptionally strong sense of hearing, but to also be blind.
613 *jack*  Knave, a dishonest or unscrupulous man.

**Trinculo**  Monster, I do smell all horse-piss, at which my nose is in great
   indignation.

**Stephano**  So is mine. Do you hear, monster? If I should take a displeasure          200
   against you, look you—

**Trinculo**  Thou wert but a lost monster.

**Caliban**  Good my lord, give me thy favour still.
   Be patient, for the prize I'll bring thee to
   Shall hoodwink this mischance. [614] Therefore speak softly.          205
   All's hushed as midnight yet.

**Trinculo**  Aye, but to lose our bottles in the pool!

**Stephano**  There is not only disgrace and dishonour in that, monster, but an
   infinite loss.

**Trinculo**  That's more to me than my wetting;[615] yet this is your harmless fairy,          210
   monster.

**Stephano**  I will fetch off my bottle, though I be o'er ears for my labour.[616]

**Caliban**  Prithee, my king, be quiet. See'st thou here,
   This is the mouth o' th' cell. No noise, and enter.
   Do that good mischief which may make this island          215
   Thine own forever, and I, thy Caliban,
   For aye thy foot-licker.

**Stephano**  Give me thy hand. I do begin to have bloody thoughts.

**Trinculo**  O King Stephano! O peer![617] O worthy Stephano! Look what a
   wardrobe here is for thee!          220

**Caliban**  Let it alone, thou fool; it is but trash.

**Trinculo**  O, ho, monster! We know what belongs to a frippery.[618]

   [*He takes a robe from the line.*]

   O King Stephano!

**Stephano**  Put off that gown, Trinculo. By this hand, I'll have that gown.

**Trinculo**  Thy grace[619] shall have it.          225

---

614  *hoodwink this mischance*  "Shall make you forget this trifling misfortune. To hoodwink is to
   blindfold and hence, to keep one from seeing it" (Stevenson, *The Tempest*, 112).

615  *wetting*  Being made wet.

616  *o'er ears . . . labour*  Stephano is going to go get the bottle that he lost in the swamp, even if
   he has to dive under water (over his ears) to get it.

617  *O King . . . peer*  A musical reference to a song that began "King Stephen was a worthy
   peer," sung by Iago in *Othello* (2.3.82).

618  *frippery*  Second-hand clothing shop.

619  *grace*  An honorific reserved for royalty.

**Caliban** The dropsy[620] drown this fool! What do you mean
    To dote thus on such luggage?[621] Let't alone
    And do the murder first. If he awake,
    From toe to crown he'll fill our skins with pinches,
    Make us strange stuff.      230
**Stephano** Be you quiet, monster. Mistress Line, is not this my jerkin?[622]

    [*Takes the jerkin from the line.*]

    Now is the jerkin under the line. Now, jerkin, you are like to lose your hair
    and prove a bald jerkin.[623]
**Trinculo** Do, do.[624] We steal by line and level,[625] an't[626] likeyour grace.
**Stephano** I thank thee for that jest: here's a garment for't.      235

    [*Takes a garment from the line and gives it to TRINCULO.*]

    Wit shall not go unrewarded while I am king of this country. "Steal by line
    and level" is an excellent pass of pate.[627] [*Takes another garment from the
    line.*] There's another garment for't.
**Trinculo** Monster, come, put some lime upon your fingers, and away with the
    rest.      240
**Caliban** I will have none on't. We shall lose our time,
    And all be turned to barnacles,[628] or to apes
    With foreheads villainous[629] low.
**Stephano** Monster, lay to[630] your fingers. Help to bear this away where my
    hogshead of wine is, or I'll turn you out of my kingdom. Go to, carry this.      245
**Trinculo** And this.
**Stephano** Aye, and this.

---

620  *dropsy*  A disease characterized by swelling of the joints due to accumulation of watery fluid.
621  *luggage*  Encumbrances, burdens.
622  *jerkin*  A kind of jacket.
623  *Now is . . . jerkin*  It was thought that travellers who went below the equator, due to the
    length of the voyage, would inevitably get sick and lose their hair. Also, if Stephano is refer-
    ring to his own body (tucking the jerkin in), it could be a reference to syphilis as that disease
    was thought to cause heat in the genitals that rid the body of hair.
624  *Do, do*  Bravo.
625  *line and level*  Carpenter's level and plumb line; they are expert thieves.
626  *an't*  And it.
627  *pass of pate*  Thrust of wit. Pate was a contemptuous term for head.
628  *barnacles*  Either the shellfish or the barnacle goose, which was thought to emerge from the
    shellfish.
629  *villainous*  Vilely, wretchedly.
630  *lay to*  Put to action.

[*They give CALIBAN the garments.*] *A noise of hunters heard. Enter divers*[631] *spirits, in shape of dogs and hounds, and hunt them about, PROSPERO and ARIEL setting them on.*

**Prospero**   Hey, Mountain, hey!
**Ariel**   Silver! There it goes, Silver!
**Prospero**   Fury, Fury! There, Tyrant,[632] there! Hark! Hark!                    250
   Go charge[633] my goblins[634] that they grind their joints
   With dry convulsions, shorten up their sinews
   With aged cramps, and more pinch-spotted[635] make them
   Than pard[636] or cat o' mountain.
**Ariel**                                        Hark, they roar!
**Prospero**   Let them be hunted soundly. At this hour                    255
   Lies at my mercy all mine enemies.
   Shortly shall all my labours end, and thou
   Shalt have the air at freedom. For a little,
   Follow and do me service.

                                        [*Exeunt.*]

# ACT FIVE, SCENE ONE (5.1)

In the final scene, the three different storylines are brought together and, beyond all expectation, PROSPERO forgives his villainous brother, ANTONIO, for stealing his dukedom. As the scene opens, PROSPERO appears in his full magic robes with ARIEL and asks that ARIEL summon the courtiers before him. While alone on stage, PROSPERO vows that he will give up his magic, using a speech that was apparently glossed from an earlier writer, Ovid.

ARIEL returns with the Neapolitans under a spell and PROSPERO momentarily revels in the power he has over his enemies. PROSPERO then orders ARIEL to bring the BOATSWAIN from the ship to them. Eventually, the spell begins to break and the courtiers become aware of where they are. PROSPERO first

---

631   *divers*   Many.
632   *Mountain ... Tyrant*   "Mountain," "Silver," "Fury," and "Tyrant" are all names of dogs the
         spirits are impersonating.
633   *charge*   Order.
634   *goblins*   Spirits.
635   *pinch-spotted*   Bruised.
636   *pard*   Leopard.

hugs GONZALO, then subtly threatens ANTONIO and SEBASTIAN. In the key moment of reconciliation in the play, PROSPERO forgives ANTONIO for his usurpation of his dukedom. This moment is all too often played as a foregone conclusion, but it must be remembered that PROSPERO suggests repeatedly in the play that his powers are such that he will take vengeance on his brother, not reconcile with him and show mercy. Finally, PROSPERO commiserates with ALONSO. The king claims to have lost his son in the storm, while PROSPERO claims to have lost his daughter.

Then, PROSPERO reveals FERDINAND and MIRANDA playing chess (where FERDINAND is cheating). Father and son are happily reunited and MIRANDA is amazed to see so many new faces.

The BOATSWAIN is led onstage by ARIEL and reveals that the ship, which appeared to sink in the storm, is actually seaworthy and hidden in a nearby cove.

Finally, CALIBAN, TRINCULO, and STEPHANO appear onstage and are brought to justice. CALIBAN remains a servant while STEPHANO and TRINCULO are given over to ALONSO for punishment. ALONSO asks for an explanation of these strange events and PROSPERO promises to give one afterwards. Everyone but PROSPERO goes into the cell, leaving PROSPERO alone onstage.

In the epilogue, PROSPERO asks for the approval of the audience and surrenders his magical powers.

## Act Five
### Scene One

*Enter PROSPERO in his magic robes, and ARIEL.*

**Prospero**  Now does my project gather to a head.
My charms crack not, my spirits obey, and Time
Goes upright with his carriage.[637] How's the day?
**Ariel**  On[638] the sixth hour, at which time, my lord,
You said our work should cease.
**Prospero**                                    I did say so,                     5
When first I raised the tempest. Say, my spirit,
How fares the king and's followers?

---

637  *Time / Goes . . . carriage*  Time walks without bending (goes upright) because the weight he carries (his carriage) has been lifted. The weight here is the anticipation of future events.
638  *On*  Near.

**Ariel**                                    Confined together
In the same fashion as you gave in charge,
Just as you left them; all prisoners, sir,
In the line grove which weather-fends your cell.[639]                    10
They cannot budge till your release. The king,
His brother, and yours, abide[640] all three distracted,[641]
And the remainder mourning over them,
Brimful of sorrow and dismay; but chiefly
Him that you termed, sir, the good old Lord Gonzalo,                    15
His tears run down his beard, like winter's drops
From eaves of reeds.[642] Your charm so strongly works 'em
That if you now beheld them, your affections[643]
Would become tender.
**Prospero**                    Dost thou think so, spirit?
**Ariel** Mine would, sir, were I human.
**Prospero**                                And mine shall.                    20
Hast thou, which art but air, a touch,[644] a feeling
Of their afflictions, and shall not myself,
One of their kind, that relish all as sharply,
Passion as they,[645] be kindlier moved[646] than thou art?
Though with their high wrongs I am struck to th' quick,[647]              25
Yet with my nobler reason 'gainst my fury
Do I take part. The rarer[648] action is
In virtue than in vengeance. They being penitent,

---

639  *In the . . . cell*  In the grove of trees that serves as a windbreak outside your home.
640  *abide*  Remain.
641  *distracted*  Preoccupied, unfocused; troubled, upset; mad.
642  *eaves of reeds*  Thatched roofs.
643  *affections*  Inclinations, passions; also, the actions that influence the mind. This secondary sense draws on the discourse of rhetoric where an "affection" was an action used to bring about a mental state in another. To "affect" in Shakespeare could mean to love, to like, to be pleased with.
644  *touch*  Feeling.
645  *that relish . . . they*  "That enjoy (relish) pleasure just as keenly, and feel sorrow (passion) in the same way as they. *Passion* is a verb. If we omit the comma after *sharply*, 'passion' must be considered as a noun, object of *relish*. Some editors prefer this reading" (Stevenson, *The Tempest*, 115).
646  *kindlier moved*  More sympathetically affected.
647  *struck to . . . quick*  Proverbial, drawn from fencing discourse, where "the quick" is the flesh beneath the fingernail. To cut an opponent's nail and strike the quick was extremely difficult, and, for the opponent, extremely painful. Thus, to strike to the quick is to have a strong emotional effect, to get at the central or most sensitive part of someone or something.
648  *rarer*  More unusual, finer.

The sole drift[649] of my purpose doth extend
Not a frown further. Go release them, Ariel.                                    30
My charms I'll break, their senses I'll restore,
And they shall be themselves.
**Ariel**                                   I'll fetch them, sir.

[*Exit.*]

**Prospero** Ye elves of hills, brooks, standing lakes, and groves,
And ye that on the sands with printless foot[650]
Do chase the ebbing Neptune, and do fly[651] him                               35
When he comes back; you demi-puppets[652] that
By moonshine do the green sour ringlets[653] make,
Whereof the ewe not bites;[654] and you whose pastime
Is to make midnight mushrooms,[655] that rejoice
To hear the solemn curfew;[656] by whose aid—                                  40
Weak masters though ye be—I have bedimmed[657]
The noontide sun, called forth the mutinous winds,
And 'twixt the green sea and the azured vault[658]
Set roaring war;[659] to the dread rattling thunder
Have I given fire,[660] and rifted Jove's stout oak                            45
With his own bolt; the strong-based promontory
Have I made shake, and by the spurs plucked up
The pine and cedar. Graves at my command
Have waked their sleepers, oped, and let 'em forth[661]
By my so potent art. But this rough magic                                      50
I here abjure;[662] and when I have required[663]
Some heavenly music—which even now I do—

---

649  *drift*  Tendency or intention.
650  *printless foot*  Leaving no trace or footprint.
651  *fly*  Run away from.
652  *demi-puppets*  A half-sized puppet; an elf.
653  *green sour ringlets*  Rings that appear in grass, caused by mushrooms.
654  *ewe not bites*  Sheep won't eat sour grass.
655  *midnight mushrooms*  Thought to grow so quickly due to the influence of fairies.
656  *solemn curfew*  The curfew bell, at nine o'clock, when spirits were thought to roam.
657  *bedimmed*  Darkened.
658  *azured vault*  The sky.
659  *Set roaring war*  Created tempests.
660  *fire*  Lightning.
661  *Graves at . . . forth*  Necromancy. This is the only admission of necromancy or black magic in
     the whole of the play, which perhaps suggests why Prospero must give up his art.
662  *abjure*  Give up.
663  *required*  Demanded.

To work mine end upon their senses that
This airy charm is for, I'll break my staff,
Bury it certain fathoms in the earth,[664]                                    55
And deeper than did ever plummet sound
I'll drown my book.[665]

*Solemn music.*

*Enter ARIEL as before; then ALONSO, with a frantic gesture, attended
by GONZALO; SEBASTIAN and ANTONIO in like manner, attended by
ADRIAN and FRANCISCO. They all enter the circle which PROSPERO had
made, and there stand charmed, which PROSPERO observing, speaks:*

A solemn air, and the best comforter
To an unsettled fancy,[666] cure thy brains,
Now useless, boil within thy skull! There stand,                            60
For you are spell-stopped.[667]
Holy Gonzalo, honourable man,
Mine eyes, ev'n sociable to the show of thine,
Fall fellowly drops.[668] The charm dissolves apace,[669]
And as the morning steals upon the night,                                   65
Melting the darkness, so their rising senses
Begin to chase the ignorant fumes that mantle[670]
Their clearer reason.[671] O good Gonzalo,

---

664  *I'll break . . . earth* Prospero will break and bury his staff to ensure no one else can use it.
665  *Ye elves . . . book* This whole speech is cribbed from Arthur Golding's 1567 translation
     of Ovid's *Metamorphoses*, an ancient Roman book that told the stories of mythical bodily
     transformations. In Ovid, this particular speech is in the mouth of Medea, a witch who kills her
     children to get back at her husband, who has left her for another woman. Shakespeare prunes
     the speech as it appears in Ovid so as to remove most of the references to black magic, yet,
     as noted above, necromancy remains indelibly present in the sense of the lines. Golding's
     translation was well-known, thus Shakespeare seems to be deliberately citing it in this speech.
     Why would Shakespeare do this?
666  *unsettled fancy* Troubled imagination.
667  *spell-stopped* Under a spell.
668  *Fall fellowly drops* Cry sympathetic tears.
669  *apace* Quickly.
670  *mantle* Cover.
671  *rising senses . . . reason* "Their power to perceive and understand is returning, and the mad-
     ness which kept them in ignorance of what was going on and prevented them from reasoning
     clearly, is being chased away. The figure is taken from chemistry. The confusion in their minds
     is compared to a scum (mantle) which is being driven off in the form of heavy gas (fumes) by
     some chemical action" (Stevenson, *The Tempest*, 116). This note by Stevenson provides a
     uniquely scientific reading of the image, which was in keeping with the early modern under-
     standing of magic. That is, science and magic were largely indistinguishable at the time. Thus,
     Prospero's magic draws on what we today would think of as scientific discourse.

My true preserver, and a loyal sir[672]
To him[673] you follow'st, I will pay thy graces                        70
Home both in word and deed! Most cruelly
Did'st thou, Alonso, use me and my daughter.
Thy brother was a furtherer in the act—
Thou art pinched[674] for't now, Sebastian![675] Flesh and blood,
You, brother mine, that entertained ambition,                          75
Expelled remorse and nature; who, with Sebastian—
Whose inward pinches therefore are most strong—
Would here have killed your king, I do forgive thee,
Unnatural though thou art. Their understanding
Begins to swell, and the approaching tide                              80
Will shortly fill the reasonable shore,
That now lies foul and muddy. Not one of them
That yet looks on me, or would know me. Ariel,
Fetch me the hat and rapier[676] in my cell.

> [*Exit ARIEL who immediately returns.*]

I will discase[677] me, and myself present                             85
As I was sometime Milan. Quickly, spirit!
Thou shalt ere long be free.

*ARIEL sings and helps to attire him.*

**Ariel**    Where the bee sucks, there suck I,
          In a cowslip's bell[678] I lie;
          There I couch[679] when owls do cry;                         90
          On the bat's back I do fly
          After summer merrily.
          Merrily, merrily shall I live now
          Under the blossom that hangs on the bough.

---

672  *sir*  Gentleman.
673  *him*  Alonso.
674  *pinched*  Tormented; also, blamed or criticized (*OED*, 3rd ed., v11b).
675  *Thy brother . . . Sebastian*  This is the first time Shakespeare tells the audience that Sebastian was complicit in the plot to remove Prospero from his dukedom. Why wait so late to reveal this to the audience?
676  *hat and rapier*  A rapier was a kind of sword. Most Renaissance gentleman would have sported these as part of their everyday wear.
677  *discase*  Undress.
678  *cowslip's bell*  The flower of a cowslip, the *Primula veris*, which hangs downwards. According to Gerard's *Herbal*, cowslip flowers were useful to ease cramps and diseases of the sinews (783).
679  *couch*  Lay down, rest, crouch.

**Prospero** Why, that's my dainty Ariel! I shall miss thee,                    95
    But yet thou shalt have freedom. So, so, so.[680]
    To the king's ship, invisible as thou art;
    There shalt thou find the mariners asleep
    Under the hatches.[681] The Master and the Boatswain
    Being awake,[682] enforce them to this place,                    100
    And presently,[683] I prithee.
**Ariel** I drink the air before me,[684] and return
    Or ere your pulse twice beat.

                                                   [*Exit.*]

**Gonzalo** All torment, trouble, wonder, and amazement
    Inhabits here. Some heavenly power guide us                    105
    Out of this fearful country!
**Prospero** Behold, sir king,
    The wronged Duke of Milan, Prospero.
    For more assurance that a living prince
    Does now speak to thee, I embrace thy body,                    110
    And to thee and thy company I bid
    A hearty welcome.
**Alonso** Whe'er[685] thou be'st he or no,
    Or some enchanted trifle[686] to abuse[687] me,
    As late I have been, I not know. Thy pulse                    115
    Beats as of flesh and blood; and, since I saw thee,
    Th' affliction of my mind amends, with which,
    I fear, a madness held me. This must crave,[688]
    An if this be at all, a most strange story.
    Thy dukedom I resign[689] and do entreat                    120

---

680  *So, so, so*  This is an example of the rhetorical trope *epizeuxis*, which is the emphatic repetition of the same word with no other words between. It is used to create emotional intensity, but also has the effect of slowing down the tempo of a scene or speech as a result of the caesuras or stops (here commas) that separate the repeated word.
681  *under the hatches*  Below deck.
682  *being awake*  When you have woken them.
683  *presently*  Quickly.
684  *drink the air*  Proverbial. To move exceptionally quickly.
685  *Whe'er*  Whether.
686  *enchanted trifle*  Conjured apparition.
687  *abuse*  Mistreat.
688  *This must crave*  Your presence is so impossible that it demands.
689  *resign*  Milan, after Prospero's usurpation, was a vassal of Naples. Alonso gives up his rights over Milan.

Thou pardon me my wrongs. But how should[690] Prospero
Be living, and be here?
**Prospero**                          First, noble friend,
Let me embrace thine age, whose honour cannot
Be measured or confined.

[*Embraces GONZALO.*]

**Gonzalo**                          Whether this be,
Or be not, I'll not swear.
**Prospero**                          You do yet taste                          125
Some subtleties o' th' isle, that will not let you
Believe things certain. Welcome, my friends all!

[*Aside to SEBASTIAN and ANTONIO.*]

But you, my brace[691] of lords, were I so minded,
I here could pluck[692] his highness' frown upon you
And justify[693] you traitors. At this time                          130
I will tell no tales.
**Sebastian**                          The devil speaks in him!
**Prospero**                                                  No.
For you, most wicked sir, whom to call brother
Would even infect my mouth, I do forgive
Thy rankest fault—all of them—and require
My dukedom of thee, which perforce[694] I know                          135
Thou must restore.[695]
**Alonso**                          If thou be'st Prospero,
Give us particulars[696] of thy preservation;
How thou hast met us here, who three hours since[697]

---

690  *how should*  How is it possible?
691  *brace*  Pair, subtly drawing on hunting discourse. A brace was a reference to kinds of game
        strung together (a brace of fish or of ducks). Prospero is implying that Sebastian and Antonio
        are his prey, further complicating his character and especially his benevolence.
692  *pluck*  Bring down.
694  *justify*  Prove.
694  *perforce*  By necessity.
695  *No. / For . . . restore*  This whole speech can be seen as the crux of Prospero's character and
        the moment when he lets go of the anger that he has been harbouring for the whole play and
        gives over to the Christian virtue of mercy.
696  *particulars*  The details.
697  *three hours since*  *The Tempest*, unique among Shakespeare's plays, attempts to follow the
        Aristotelian "Unities." Aristotle theorized that a drama should take place in a single place
        (the island), with a single plot (the story of Prospero getting his dukedom back), and in a span
        of time equal to the amount of time it takes to watch the play. The play takes approximately
        three hours to stage.

Were wrecked upon this shore, where I have lost—
How sharp the point of this remembrance is!—                    140
My dear son Ferdinand.

**Prospero**                    I am woe[698] for't, sir.

**Alonso** Irreparable is the loss, and patience
Says it is past her cure.[699]

**Prospero**                    I rather think
You have not sought her help, of whose soft grace
For the like loss[700] I have her sovereign aid,                    145
And rest myself content.

**Alonso**                    You the like loss?

**Prospero** As great to me as late;[701] and supportable
To make the dear loss, have I means much weaker
Than you may call to comfort you, for I
Have lost my daughter.

**Alonso**                    A daughter?                    150
O heavens, that they were living both in Naples,
The king and queen there! That they were, I wish
Myself were mudded[702] in that oozy bed
Where my son lies. When did you lose your daughter?

**Prospero** In this last tempest. I perceive these lords                    155
At this encounter do so much admire
That they devour their reason and scarce think
Their eyes do offices of truth.[703] Their words
Are natural breath.[704] But, howsoe'er you have
Been jostled from your senses, know for certain                    160
That I am Prospero and that very duke
Which was thrust forth of[705] Milan, who most strangely
Upon this shore, where you were wrecked, was landed
To be the lord on't.[706] No more yet of this,
For 'tis a chronicle of day by day,[707]                    165

---

698  *woe*  Sorry.
699  *past her cure*  Beyond her capacity to cure.
700  *the like loss*  Prospero claims to have lost his daughter, which is figuratively true insofar as she is to be married to Ferdinand.
701  *late*  Recent
702  *mudded*  Buried in the mud.
703  *offices of truth*  Report the truth.
704  *natural breath*  Ordinary speech; also, honest speech.
705  *of*  From.
706  *on't*  Of it.
707  *day by day*  To be told over many days.

Not a relation[708] for a breakfast, nor
Befitting this first meeting. Welcome, sir;
This cell's my court. Here have I few attendants,
And subjects none abroad. Pray you look in.
My dukedom since you have given me again,                   170
I will requite you with as good a thing,
At least bring forth a wonder, to content ye
As much as me my dukedom.

*Here PROSPERO discovers FERDINAND and MIRANDA*
*playing at chess.*

***Miranda***  Sweet lord, you play me false.[709]
***Ferdinand***                                  No, my dearest love,
I would not for the world.                                  175
***Miranda***  Yes, for a score[710] of kingdoms you should wrangle,[711]
And I would call it fair play.[712]
***Alonso***                          If this prove
A vision of the island, one dear son
Shall I twice lose.
***Sebastian***           A most high miracle!
***Ferdinand***  Though the seas threaten, they are merciful.   180
I have cursed them without cause.

*[FERDINAND kneels.]*

***Alonso***  Now all the blessings
Of a glad father compass thee about![713]
Arise, and say how thou cam'st here.

*[FERDINAND rises.]*

***Miranda***  O, wonder!                                       185
How many goodly creatures are there here?

---

708  *relation*  Story.
709  *play me false*  Ferdinand is cheating.
710  *score*  Twenty.
711  *wrangle*  Dispute, bargain, debate, bicker.
712  *score of . . . play*  "Ferdinand has just said that he wouldn't cheat for the world. In reply
      Miranda jestingly puns on the word score in the sense of the score in the game, and the score
      as a number. In chess the player who captures his opponent's king, wins the game, and thus,
      in a sense, they are playing for a kingdom" (Stevenson, *The Tempest*, 118).
713  *compass thee about*  Embrace you.

How beauteous mankind[714] is?[715]! O brave new world,
That has such people in't.

**Prospero**                               'Tis new to thee.

**Alonso**  What is this maid with whom thou wast at play?
Your eld'st acquaintance cannot be three hours.                    190
Is she the goddess that hath severed us,
And brought us thus together?

**Ferdinand**                         Sir, she is mortal;
But by immortal Providence she's mine.
I chose her when I could not ask my father
For his advice: nor thought I had one. She                         195
Is daughter to this famous Duke of Milan,
Of whom so often I have heard renown,[716]
But never saw before; of whom I have
Received a second life; and second father
This lady makes him to me.

**Alonso**                         I am hers.[717]                  200
But O, how oddly will it sound that I
Must ask my child forgiveness!

**Prospero**                         There, sir, stop.
Let us not burthen our remembrance with
A heaviness[718] that's gone.

**Gonzalo**                         I have inly[719] wept,
Or should have spoke ere this: look down, you gods,                205
And on this couple drop a blessed crown;[720]
For it is you that have chalked forth[721] the way
Which brought us hither.

---

714  *mankind*  Humankind.

715  *?*  Most editions do not put this as a question, yet the Folio has a question mark after this statement. It could well be a compositor's error, but this edition has chosen to offer the possibility that Miranda is asking if this is "how beauteous" humanity really is. In early modern English, the pronoun "this" could be dropped if the referent was self-evident. In other words, "is humanity (really) this beautiful?"

716  *renown*  Report.

717  *hers*  Her father.

718  *heaviness*  Sadness.

719  *inly*  Inwardly.

720  *crown*  The united crowns of Naples and Milan. There are multiple levels of contextual meaning possible, however. The play was originally performed at the wedding of Princess Elizabeth, daughter of James VI/I, to the Elector Palatine of the Holy Roman Empire, thus uniting the two Protestant houses and nations. Further, James himself united the crowns of England and Scotland when he ascended to the throne of England in 1603.

721  *chalked forth*  Marked the trail, as if with chalk.

**Alonso**  I say Amen, Gonzalo!

**Gonzalo**  Was Milan[722] thrust from Milan, that his issue                     210
    Should become Kings of Naples? O, rejoice
    Beyond a common joy, and set it down
    With gold on lasting pillars! In one voyage
    Did Claribel her husband find at Tunis,
    And Ferdinand, her brother, found a wife                           215
    Where he himself was lost, Prospero his dukedom
    In a poor isle, and all of us ourselves
    When no man was his own.

**Alonso**  [*To FERDINAND and MIRANDA.*]
                       Give me your hands.
    Let grief and sorrow still[723] embrace his heart
    That doth not wish you joy!

**Gonzalo**                Be't[724] so! Amen!                     220

*Enter ARIEL, with the MASTER and BOATSWAIN amazedly following.*

    O, look, sir, look, sir! Here is more of us!
    I prophesied if a gallows were on land,
    This fellow could not drown. Now, blasphemy,
    That swear'st grace o'erboard, not an oath on shore?
    Hast thou no mouth by land?[725] What is the news?                  225

**Boatswain**  The best news is that we have safely found
    Our king and company; the next, our ship,
    Which but three glasses[726] since we gave out split,[727]
    Is tight and yare[728] and bravely rigged as when
    We first put out to sea.

**Ariel**  [*Aside to PROSPERO.*]
                     Sir, all this service                          230
    Have I done since I went.

**Prospero**  [*Aside to ARIEL.*]
                 My tricksy[729] spirit!

---

722  *Milan*  The Duke of Milan, Prospero.
723  *still*  Always.
724  *Be't*  Be it.
725  *Hast thou . . . land*  Can you not speak on shore?
726  *glasses*  Hours, after the hourglass that was kept on board sailing ships.
727  *gave out split*  Reported wrecked.
728  *tight and yare*  Seaworthy.
729  *tricksy*  Playful.

**Alonso**  These are not natural events, they strengthen[730]
　　From strange to stranger. Say, how came you hither?
**Boatswain**  If I did think, sir, I were well awake,
　　I'ld[731] strive to tell you. We were dead of sleep,[732]          235
　　And—how we know not—all clapped under hatches,
　　Where but e'en now with strange and several noises
　　Of roaring, shrieking, howling, jingling chains,
　　And more diversity of sounds, all horrible,
　　We were awaked, straightway, at liberty,          240
　　Where we, in all our trim,[733] freshly beheld
　　Our royal, good and gallant ship; our master
　　Cap'ring[734] to eye her—on a trice,[735] so please you,
　　Even in a dream, were we divided from them,[736]
　　And were brought moping[737] hither.
**Ariel**  [*Aside to PROSPERO.*]
　　　　　　　　　　　　　　　　Was't well done?          245
**Prospero**  [*Aside to ARIEL.*]
　　Bravely, my diligence. Thou shalt be free.
**Alonso**  This is as strange a maze as e'er men trod
　　And there is in this business more than nature
　　Was ever conduct[738] of. Some oracle
　　Must rectify our knowledge.
**Prospero**　　　　　　　　　Sir, my liege,          250
　　Do not infest your mind with beating on
　　The strangeness of this business. At picked leisure
　　Which shall be shortly single, I'll resolve you,
　　Which to you shall seem probable, of every
　　These happened accidents;[739] till when, be cheerful          255
　　And think of each thing well.

---

730 *strengthen*  Grow.
731 *I'ld*  An early form of the contraction of I would.
732 *dead of sleep*  Deep asleep.
733 *trim*  Garments.
734 *Cap'ring*  Dancing with joy.
735 *on a trice*  A "trice" is a pulley, and "on a trice" is literally at a single pull of the pulley. Figuratively it means very fast.
736 *them*  The other members of the crew.
737 *moping*  Confused. To mope in Shakespeare had the sense of being in a state of unconsciousness, to move or act without the impulse or guidance of thought (Schmidt, *Shakespeare Lexicon*, vol. 2 737).
738 *conduct*  Conductor, director, manager; also, conduit or conveyance.
739 *accidents*  Events.

[*Aside to ARIEL.*]

Come hither, spirit:
Set Caliban and his companions free;
Untie the spell.

[*Exit ARIEL.*]

How fares my gracious sir?
There are yet missing of your company
Some few odd lads that you remember not.                              260

*Enter ARIEL, driving in CALIBAN, STEPHANO, and TRINCULO, in their*
*stolen apparel.*

**Stephano**  Every man shift for all the rest,[740] and let no man take care for him
self, for all is but fortune. *Coraggio*, bully-monster, *coraggio!* [741]
**Trinculo**  If these be true spies which I wear in my head, here's a goodly sight.
**Caliban**  O Setebos, these be brave spirits indeed.
How fine my master is! I am afraid                                    265
He will chastise me.
**Sebastian**  Ha, ha!
What things are these, my lord Antonio?
Will money buy 'em?
**Antonio**                    Very like. One of them
Is a plain fish, and, no doubt marketable.                            270
**Prospero**  Mark but the badges[742] of these men, my lords,
Then say if they be true. This misshapen knave,
His mother was a witch, and one so strong
That could control the moon, make flows and ebbs,
And deal in her command without her power.                            275
These three have robbed me; and this demi-devil—
For he's a bastard one—had plotted with them
To take my life. Two of these fellows you
Must know and own; this thing of darkness I
Acknowledge mine.[743]

---

740  *Every man . . . rest*  Stephano is so drunk and confused that he has inverted his meaning.
     Every man for himself.
741  *Corragio*  Italian for "Courage."
742  *badges*  As servants of the royal household, they would be wearing a servant's uniform or livery.
743  *Acknowledge mine*  It is possible that this is the moment of self-knowledge or *anagnorisis*
     that was demanded by Renaissance followers of Aristotle's theories on drama. In such a
     reading, Prospero recognizes that he is responsible for Caliban's welfare, spiritually as well as
     physically.

*Caliban*                    I shall be pinched to death!                    280
*Alonso*  Is not this Stephano, my drunken butler?
*Sebastian*  He is drunk now—where had he wine?
*Alonso*  And Trinculo is reeling-ripe![744] Where should they
    Find this grand liquor that hath gilded 'em?
    How cam'st thou in this pickle?                    285
*Trinculo*  I have been in such a pickle[745] since I saw you last that, I fear me, will
    never out of my bones. I shall not fear fly-blowing.[746]
*Sebastian*  Why, how now, Stephano?
*Stephano*  O, touch me not; I am not Stephano, but a cramp.
*Prospero*  You'd be king o' the isle, sirrah?[747]                    290
*Stephano*  I should have been a sore one then.
*Alonso*  This is a strange thing as e'er I looked on.

    [*Pointing to CALIBAN.*]

*Prospero*  He is as disproportioned in his manners
    As in his shape. Go, sirrah, to my cell;
    Take with you your companions. As you look[748]                    295
    To have my pardon, trim it handsomely.[749]
*Caliban*  Aye, that I will; and I'll be wise hereafter,
    And seek for grace. What a thrice-double[750] ass
    Was I to take this drunkard for a god
    And worship this dull fool!
*Prospero*                    Go to, away!                    300
*Alonso*  Hence, and bestow your luggage where you found it.
*Sebastian*  Or stole it, rather.

    [*Exeunt CALIBAN, STEPHANO, and TRINCULO.*]

*Prospero*  Sir, I invite your highness and your train[751]
    To my poor cell, where you shall take your rest
    For this one night, which part of it I'll waste[752]                    305

---

744  *reeling-ripe*  So drunk he cannot stand, severely inebriated.
745  *pickle*  Both meaning that he has been so drunk, and that he has been in such trouble.
746  *fly-blowing*  He's had so much to drink (he smells so bad) that flies won't even lay their eggs
    on him.
747  *sirrah*  A contemptuous form of address.
748  *look*  Hope.
749  *trim it handsomely*  Despite Prospero's admission of responsibility for Caliban's welfare,
    Caliban remains firmly his slave.
750  *thrice-double*  Six times over.
751  *train*  Group of counsellors (Gonzalo and the rest).
752  *waste*  Spend.

With such discourse as I not doubt shall make it
Go quick away: the story of my life
And the particular accidents gone by
Since I came to this isle; and in the morn
I'll bring you to your ship, and so to Naples,⁣ 310
Where I have hope to see the nuptial
Of these our dear-beloved solemnized,
And thence retire me to my Milan, where
Every third thought shall be my grave.⁷⁵³
**Alonso**⁣ I long
To hear the story of your life, which must⁣ 315
Take the ear⁷⁵⁴ strangely.
**Prospero**⁣ I'll deliver all,
And promise you calm seas, auspicious gales
And sail so expeditious that shall catch
Your royal fleet far off.

[*Aside to ARIEL.*]

⁣ My Ariel, chick,⁷⁵⁵
That is thy charge. Then to the elements⁣ 320
Be free, and fare thou well! Please you, draw near.

⁣ [*Exeunt omnes.*]

# EPILOGUE

*Spoken by PROSPERO.*

Now my charms are all o'erthrown,
And what strength I have's mine own,
Which is most faint. Now, 'tis true,
I must be here confined by you,⁷⁵⁶
Or sent to Naples. Let me not,⁣ 5

---

753 *Every third . . . grave* "I shall prepare myself, by contemplation, for death" (Stevenson, *The Tempest*, 120). In many ways, this is a conventional *memento mori* trope, or remembrance of death. Orgel, however, suggests "Prospero has now arranged matters so that his death will remove Antonio's last link with the ducal power. His grave is the ultimate triumph over his brother." Stephen Orgel, *The Tempest* (New York: Oxford, 1987), 55.
754 *Take the ear* Affect the listener.
755 *chick* A diminutive and also a term of endearment.
756 *you* The audience.

Since I have my dukedom got,
And pardoned the deceiver, dwell
In this bare island by your spell,
But release me from my bands
With the help of your good hands.[757]          10
Gentle breath of yours my sails
Must fill, or else my project fails,
Which was to please. Now I want[758]
Spirits to enforce, art to enchant,
And my ending is despair                        15
Unless I be relieved by prayer,
Which pierces so that it assaults
Mercy itself and frees all faults.
As you from crimes would pardoned be,
Let your indulgence[759] set me free.            20

[*Exit.*]

---

757 *release me . . . hands* Referring to the confinement on stage of both actor and character.
Prospero and actor are both confined to the island/stage until the audience applauds.
758 *want* Lack.
759 *indulgence* Favour. Also, within Roman Catholicism, a remission of sin granted by the Church
for payment, one of the prime causes of the Lutheran Reformation in Europe. Both meanings
would have been resonant to Shakespeare's audience.

# Oxford Shakespeare Made in Canada Series: Statement on Editorial Principles and Works Cited

These editions have been newly prepared by a team of researchers associated with the Canadian Adaptations of Shakespeare Project at the University of Guelph. The collation and analysis of the relevant quarto editions and of the 1623 First Folio of Shakespeare was undertaken using the following principles.

Modernization of spelling has been in accordance with Canadian English spelling, which makes use of elements of British English and American English. Thus words that end in "-our" or "-re" (such as "valour," "centre," and "colour") stand next to American spellings such as "jail" and other idiosyncratic uses specific to Canadian English. Both stressed and unstressed past participles appear in the text as "-ed." Punctuation has been likewise modernized to clarify the meaning of the text while interfering as little with the syntax as possible. Stage directions appear as they do in the original quartos and Folio texts, with clarifications appearing in square brackets. For example, exits and entrances, which are often missing in Shakespeare, have been supplied in square brackets. Occasionally, where the same character is referred to in multiple ways in the original material, these references have been standardized. Scene locations have not been supplied as per source texts and to allow readers to speculate about locations on their own. In the case of a so-called bad quarto or corrupted text, the fuller or richer reading is preferred, even if that is found in the "bad" quarto.

Editorial notes primarily gloss the Shakespearean text, explicating the meaning wherever possible and attending to issues of multiple and ambiguous meanings. Glossing of individual words has been drawn from the *Oxford English Dictionary*, Alexander Schmidt's monumental *Shakespeare Lexicon and Quotation Dictionary*, and David and Ben Crystal's *Shakespeare's Words*. Longer explanatory notes draw from a number of sources, including Shakespeare's own source materials, Morris Palmer Tilley's *A Dictionary of the Proverbs in*

*England in the Sixteenth and Seventeenth Centuries*, and previous important editions. Citations are available wherever other editions have been used, and preference has been shown for editions prepared by Canadian scholars. One set of editions of especial note for this series is that prepared between 1915 and 1943 by Orlando John (O.J.) Stevenson. Stevenson was the head of the English Department at the Ontario Agricultural College (later the University of Guelph), a prominent Canadian Shakespearean, and member of the New Education Movement. In the first half of the twentieth century he made major contributions to building a critical framework for understanding Shakespeare in Canada. His exhaustive explanatory notes in his editions have been liberally cited in all editions of this series. Many of the notes in these editions are pedagogical, even interrogative, in orientation, encouraging students to consider questions about character, text, and performance. Notes related to productions and adaptations have been drawn from the Canadian Adaptations of Shakespeare Project, also at the University of Guelph. Throughout, the aim has been to create readable, reliable, elegant, historically respectful yet modern texts that give students access to the range of tools they need to grasp the rich play of meaning to be found in Shakespeare's texts.

All the playtexts and editorial apparatuses have been newly prepared for Oxford University Press (Canada) under Daniel Fischlin as general editor of the Shakespeare Made in Canada Series, and are duly licensed to Oxford.

# Works Cited: *The Tempest*

Bullough, Geoffrey. *Narrative and Dramatic Sources of Shakespeare*. (8 vols.) New York: Routledge and Kegan Paul, 1975.

Crystal, David, and Ben Crystal. *Shakespeare's Words: A Glossary and Language Companion*. New York: Penguin, 2002.

Dent, R.W. *Shakespeare's Proverbial Language: An Index*. Berkeley, CA: University of California Press, 1981.

Furness, H.H. *The Tempest*. New Variorum Edition. Philadelphia: J. B. Lippincott Co., 1892.

Gerard, John. *The Herball or Generall Historie of Plantes, Gathered by Iohn Gerarde of London, Master in Chirugerie*. London: Adam Islip Ioice Norton and Richard Whitakers, 1633.

Orgel, Stephen. *The Tempest*. New York: Oxford, 1987.

Ovid. *The xv books of P. Ouidius Naso, entitled Metamorphosis, translated oute of Latin into English meeter by Arthur Golding Gentleman*. London: Willyam Seres, 1567.

Partridge, Eric. *Shakespeare's Bawdy*. London: Routledge, 1947.

Schmidt, Alexander. *Shakespeare Lexicon and Quotation Dictionary*. (2 vols.) Berlin: Reimer, 1902.

Stevenson, O.J. *The Tempest*. Toronto: Copp Clark, 1927.

Tilley, Morris Palmer. *A Dictionary of the Proverbs in England in the Sixteenth and Seventeenth Centuries*. Ann Arbor, MI: University of Michigan Press, 1950

# *Acknowledgements*

The Oxford Shakespeare Made in Canada Series would not have been possible without a core group of researchers, scholars, graduate and undergraduate research assistants, and the amazing staff at Oxford University Press (Canada). The Canadian Adaptations of Shakespeare Project (CASP) team at the University of Guelph played the central role in research, editorial, and logistical work associated with the series. Dr. Andrew Bretz, a post-doctoral researcher with CASP, made a remarkable contribution to the overall project, displaying equal measures of initiative, leadership, tact, and diligence—and exceptional scholarly acumen in helping shape the final look of these editions. Research assistants Jennie Hissa and Alyssa Ottema were an ongoing source of astute, hard-working support as far-flung research resources from across the country were called in and as we sought to identify the uniquely Canadian materials that have made their way into these volumes.

Staff at the University of Guelph Library, including Kathryn Harvey (Archival and Special Collections) and Wayne Johnston (Research Enterprise and Scholarly Communication), played essential roles in facilitating access to the University of Guelph's remarkable theatre archives, the largest in Canada. Contributors and essayists, including Sky Gilbert, Jill Levenson, and Daniel David Moses, remarkable Canadian voices each, generously contributed the distinctive points of view and scholarship present in these volumes. Their insightful contributions speak to the remarkable diversity of critical and creative voices in Canada and I am immensely grateful to be able to share their work in these volumes with a much wider audience. I'm also indebted to Monique Mojica for a very frank exchange about interpreting Shakespeare that helped shape some of the key editorial choices that were made early on. Dr. Kevin Hall, vice-president of research at the University of Guelph, and Dr. Alastair Summerlee, president of the University of Guelph, both provided significant support to the project for which I am deeply appreciative. Mr. Lloyd Sullivan, the Canadian owner of the Sanders Portrait of Shakespeare, graciously gave his permission to reproduce that remarkable painting as the emblematic image of the series. Mr. Sullivan also contributed his vast knowledge on Shakespearean lore to the overall project.

Finally, Jen Rubio, my intrepid editor at Oxford University Press, has shown incredible initiative, understanding, and resourcefulness from first conception through to realization. The daughter of a Shakespearean scholar and beloved teacher at the University of Guelph—to whom these editions are dedicated and whose office I currently occupy—Jen's acumen and enterprise have made this project an absolute joy to undertake. Her fortuitous involvement in the project has been a timely reminder of the infinitely delicate shape of fates, destinies, and contingencies that bring together a scholarly community.

Daniel Fischlin,
Shakespeare Made in Canada, Series General Editor

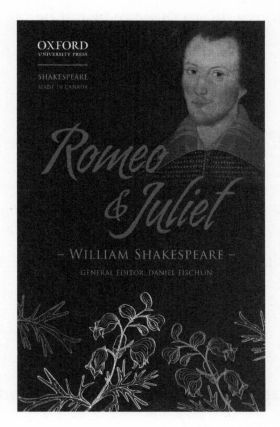

# Coming Soon

from Shakespeare Made in Canada

"*This above all: to thine own self be true.*"

*Hamlet*

"*I will wear my heart upon my sleeve.*"

*Othello*

"*Fair is foul, and foul is fair.*"

*Macbeth*

"*The course of true love never did run smooth.*"

*A Midsummer Night's Dream*

---

**SHAKESPEARE**
MADE IN CANADA